NOLS
Winter Camping

by **Buck Tilton and John Gookin**

illustrations by Joan M. Safford

STACKPOLE
BOOKS

Text copyright © 2005 by The National Outdoor Leadership School
Illustrations copyright © 1991 and 2005 by Joan M. Safford

Published by
STACKPOLE BOOKS
5067 Ritter Rd.
Mechanicsburg, PA 17055
www.stackpolebooks.com

Printed in the United States of America

10 9 8 7 6 5 4 3 2 1

First edition

Cover photograph by Marco Johnson
Cover design by Caroline Stover

Library of Congress Cataloguing-in-Publication Data
Tilton, Buck.
  NOLS winter camping / by Buck Tilton and John Gookin.
    p. cm.
  ISBN 0-8117-3183-9
  1. Snow camping. I. Title: Winter camping. II. Gookin, John. III. Title.

GV198.9.T55 2005
796.54—dc22
                                                                2004017529

Contents

Acknowledgments

A book of this nature is never the work of only one or two writers. In this case, it reflects the efforts and expertise of countless NOLS instructors who have studied and worked to make winter camping both a science and an art. It also reflects the dreams and visions of the late founder of NOLS, Paul Petzoldt, the "father of wilderness education."

Instructors Rick and Shannon Rochelle have fine-tuned the teaching of winter camping. They provided priceless information through interviews and the printed materials they have developed.

Claudia Pearson shared her time and wisdom from the seat of rations manager at NOLS, a position she has lifted to heights of perfection.

Stacy Tostrup, Marco Johnson, Drew Leemon, Pete Absolon, and Abby Warner were among the NOLS instructors who read early drafts and commented freely, adding much to the final product.

In the Admission and Marketing Department at NOLS, director Bruce Palmer held aloft the torch of vision and support, and marketing manager Jeanne O'Brien was consistently helpful and supportive.

Joan M. Safford went above and beyond the call of duty to ensure the accuracy of the illustrations in this book.

And cheers to Judith Schnell of Stackpole Books, who spent a great deal of time making sure this project happened.

Thank you all so much.

Introduction:

The Cold and the White

When something at least vaguely human first rose onto two feet, decided that it liked the view from that perspective, and became bipedal, the weather was hot. It happened somewhere near the equator, where it was (and still is) nearly always sultry. We, as a species, adapted in various ways to the heated environment of our evolutionary birth. Our virtually hairless skin is filled with abundant sweat glands, a rich source of moisture that can evaporate and cool the human exterior. We are powered by a cardiovascular system of marvelous endurance that circulates surface blood to other body parts, cooling the human interior. These adaptations allow us to endure rising seasonal heat in relative safety and comfort.

When did humanoid and snow first meet? Perhaps three million years ago in Africa on the heights of the Ruwenzori Range, or on Mount Kilimanjaro, somewhere far above the heat-swept savannas. Snow was certainly a factor in the lives of fur-clad people half a million years ago, as the great Ice Age crept across Europe. Most of those people chose to move to warmer climes, however. It was a long time before humans voluntarily lived in ice and snow. How long is not known for sure, but the fact that many European peoples do not have sun-protective skin pigmentation tells us that they have been out of the equatorial light for at least thousands of generations.

Today, when winter—the world of the cold and the white—draws us beyond the reach of fire and thermostat, we are not so well adapted to survive. Even though humans have lived—sometimes flourished—for thousands of years in regions where winter never leaves, they have not had eons to adapt physiologically. Some peoples with long cultural histories of exposure to the cold have grown shorter and chubbier, making it easier to retain body heat. Their cardiovascular systems may send warm blood to the exterior more readily, preventing fingers and toes from freezing. They may have higher-than-normal basal metabolic rates to generate more internal heat, even at rest. But they have yet to grow the dense, insulating fur or blubbery fat of arctic animals. To compensate for this lack of adaptation, humans have had to start using their brains—the only part of the body that allows us not only to exist but to live happily in winter.

There is much that is attractive about winter camping. The winter world is, for one thing, less crowded: no bugs, no bears, and seldom the burden of finding an intended campsite already claimed. Untracked powder offers endless opportunities for backcountry skiers and snowboarders. The utter silence of a landscape cloaked in splendid and pristine snow also attracts many. Visually speaking, the sharp light of the winter sun redefines the terrain and throws marvelous shadows across the otherwise featureless whiteness. New snow softens and balances the earth, rounding the ragged and smoothing the uneven; old snow becomes a form of art—cornices, sastrugi, penitentes—in a medium that only nature can sculpt. And then, most importantly for this book, there is the challenge of living (and living well) where few choose to tread. There are, no doubt, other reasons for going deep into winter, and in the end, as with all human endeavors, the why is probably a combination of urgings, some that are easy to put into words, and others that remain forever inexplicable.

NOLS Winter Camping is about humans living in temperatures from freezing to well below. It is about snow and ice. And it is about preparing and planning so that you can perform well in the cold. It is based on scientific knowledge and personal experience—specifically, the experience of instructors at the National Outdoor Leadership School, who, for almost forty years, have played, worked, and taught in extremes of cold. But more than anything else, it is about using your brain to not only enjoy but also flourish in wintry environments, about respecting cold without fearing it.

This book is divided into two main sections. Section I (chapters 1 to 3) covers the preparation that is necessary before you venture out into the cold, white world. Section II (chapters 4 to 9) covers important techniques and other considerations once you're out traveling and camping in winter. The Resources section points the way to additional information (including several other books in the NOLS library that deal with winter topics), and the Glossary defines unfamiliar terms.

The instructions in this book are not meant to substitute for training by an experienced winter camper. Neither NOLS nor Stackpole Books assumes responsibility for those who choose to travel deep into snow country. Indeed, when you venture out into winter, as always, you alone are responsible for the choices you make.

Chapter 1

Expedition Planning

The adventure that is winter camping begins someplace warm, dry, and comfortable. When you step outside into the cold, you need to be prepared, not only with adequate clothing and gear (see chapters 2 and 3) but also with knowledge. Knowledge (defined here as accumulated information) combined with experience leads to wisdom (defined here as the thoughtful application of knowledge). This book takes you along the trail to knowledge. If you're new to the outdoors in winter, that trail will necessarily be longer than if you're already a winter traveler. A mentor can speed up the journey, helping you avoid some of the typical mistakes in judgment that burden the novice. But whatever your level of ability and experience, winter camping trips will be safer, more comfortable, and probably happier if they are wisely planned.

ESTABLISHING GOALS

Group goals should be clearly established before heading out. Basic goals might include improving skiing skills, maintaining good health, practicing the principles of Leave No Trace (see Appendix), and enjoying the journey. But without adequate clarification, a group may leave on a winter trip thinking that the only goal is to reach a specific peak or complete a ski traverse. Helping group members focus on the right goals lets them appreciate the trip as a rich human experience, rather than merely as an opportunity to use the wilderness as a sports arena. The important thing is that all members of the expedition have the same basic mission—and to keep in mind that the mission might change, depending on unforeseen circumstances such as weather or health factors.

CHOOSING A TEAM

Contrary to popular belief, the best way to ruin a winter trip, or any trip, is not running into bad weather—it's choosing your companions poorly. If you've signed up for a guided or educational expedition, those choices have been made by fate.

If you're a novice, deciding who to invite on a backcountry trip may seem obvious: whatever friends are available. But as you take more trips of a demanding nature, you'll develop an appreciation for the importance of selecting the right companions. In fact, choosing your partners may be the most important decision you make.

The truth is that not everyone shares the same ambition, stamina, emotional comfort level, or personal definition of acceptable risk or discomfort. Many people learn this lesson the hard way, inviting the wrong people on a trip that turns into a disaster because not everyone is up to the trip's challenges. It's no fun for the person who can't keep up or for the party's stronger, more experienced members. And it's potentially dangerous for everyone.

To avoid problems, everyone should be actively involved in the planning of the trip. Less experienced people tend to leave decisions about the itinerary to more experienced party members, which can result in unpleasant surprises in the backcountry. But when everyone participates in the planning, everyone gets a clear idea of what's in store, and individuals can—and should—speak up if there's something they don't think they can handle. Keep in mind, however, that less experienced members of the team might overestimate their abilities, and more experienced members should steer novices toward wiser decisions.

As your adventures grow longer and more involved, your pool of partners will grow smaller—but that's good, because you should be more selective about your companions on more demanding trips. You'll be safest and most successful, and have the most fun, when you are accompanied by people who are prepared for and can handle whatever you encounter.

GATHERING INFORMATION

The twenty-first century abounds with information. How much information you'll need depends on variables such as how much you already know; where you plan to go, and for how long; and how eager you are to learn.

Although experience can be an excellent teacher, it can also be cruel, heartless, and, in the worst of circumstances, deadly. There is much to be said for gathering information as a student in a controlled environment from those who have "been there, done that." NOLS offers extended educational trips into the wild winter, providing safe, enjoyable, and profoundly informative experiences.

You can also gather a load of information by interviewing people who have made successful winter trips. If you can't count some of these people among your friends and acquaintances, you can find them at local outdoor stores, at the offices of local land managers, in organizations that promote and defend wilderness and wilderness travel, and on the Internet, to name a few sources.

Experts who work for government agencies—including the U.S. Forest Service (USFS), Bureau of Land Management (BLM), and National Park Service (NPS)—are often great sources of information. They can provide advice about winter travel in general as well as up-to-date details about conditions in specific areas (such as how low the temperature may dip and how much snow is on the ground). They may be able to direct you to other sources of information as well.

With a computer and access to billions of sites on the Internet, you have the answer to almost any question at your fingertips. You can search your way through tons of information, contact knowledgeable organizations, and order relevant books, technical clothing, and gear. You can also subscribe to news bulletins, join discussion groups, and ask for advice from just about anybody.

How-to books on winter travel and camping, guidebooks relevant to winter conditions, and narratives on specific areas are essentially extended interviews with the people who have been there. They may contain valuable information about distance, terrain, weather, campsites, and winter ecology. You don't always have to buy the books—check with friends and local libraries. Although books can add a huge amount of knowledge to your plan, a word of warning is needed: even if the book was published or updated recently, the specific information it contains could have changed. It is best to check a number of sources and compare the information.

Arguably, nothing conjures up the magic of an intended expedition more than poring over the lines and colors of a map. On a map, you can see the geographical journey before you take your first step. Maps can tell you distances, elevation gained and lost, and maximum elevation. They reveal hidden lakes—frozen in winter—and the extent of cloud-shrouded regions above timberline. USFS and BLM maps give you an overview, but they do not typically provide enough detailed topography to serve the specific needs of the winter traveler. It is better, in most cases, to rely on U.S. Geological Survey (USGS) maps; the best detail is provided by 7.5-minute quads in 1:24,000 scale. On the downside, USGS quads are often old and may not show current trails and other signs of human intervention. Commercial maps, such as Trails Illustrated, are readily available and increasingly accurate, and many trips can be planned with one or more of these. Thanks to modern technology, there is computer software that allows you to create your own custom maps, which you can spice up with notes and Xs marking the spots.

You should also check with local land managers about permits that may be required and regulations that must be followed. It's wiser to find out beforehand than to have to explain to an unhappy ranger, deep in a snowbound forest, why you are somewhere you shouldn't be.

CHOOSING A DESTINATION

Most winter travelers decide where they want to go—based on tales they've heard or photographs they've seen—and then gather information about their destination. But the converse might be true: you might gather information about several possible destinations and then decide. Whichever way you do it, if you're a newcomer to winter camping, keep it simple:

1. Set attainable goals for your first few trips—overnights not far from home, areas with which you are familiar.
2. Plan a trip with short escape routes in case you need to retreat.
3. Plan a route that will be easy to follow. Save those long off-trail expeditions until you have more experience.
4. Avoid extreme weather conditions. A "normal" winter is challenge enough. The focus should be on winter camping with style rather than simply surviving the elements.

LEADERSHIP

The great expeditions of history—Lewis and Clark, Shackleton, Amundsen, Peary—had a common component: outstanding leadership. Your intended journey may be less involved than, say, reaching the North Pole, but a good leader is still necessary for a good and safe trip.

What is a leader? Leadership at NOLS is defined as taking timely, appropriate actions that guide and support a group and help it to set and achieve its goals. Great leaders create an environment that inspires individuals and groups to achieve their full potential. Leadership arguably takes on more importance in winter than in summer. In winter, the elements are less forgiving and the group's basic activities—water acquisition, camp setup, snow travel—take more time and consideration, with less room for error. It takes more discipline than genius to camp in winter, and a well-led team travels with the organization and efficiency that winter demands.

Leadership Styles

Certain types of leadership style emerge on trips, whether planned or not. Decisions have to be made, and somebody has to make them. Any consideration given to leadership before a trip begins is time well spent. It is wise to discuss how your group plans to make decisions when faced with various situations—before you face them.

Some people enjoy having a leader who's clearly in charge—a decision-maker, an autocrat, a director. A leader using this directive style makes decisions unilaterally and announces them to the group. A directive leader takes much of the responsibility off group members' shoulders and saves the time necessary for group discussions of options. This type of leader should have more experience in a particular environment than anyone else in the group, so that he or she can translate that experience into wise decisions. For example, if the group needs to pass over a frozen river, an autocratic leader evaluates the ice and chooses where to cross. When conditions are severe, an experienced autocrat can provide great leadership. And when decisions are trivial, teams need not waste time discussing options when an autocratic leader is in charge.

When conditions are less severe or the group comprises individuals with similar skills and experience, a consultative leadership style has advantages. A consultative leader generally solicits opinions from the group and then makes the final decision. This gives all group members some input into the decision, which is the basis of democracy. Although consulting the group takes time, the ensuing discussion promotes learning, tends to result in a higher-quality decision, and empowers the team to implement the eventual decision. This approach has obvious drawbacks when danger is involved, and it's important to weigh the opinions of those with the most experience more heavily. Judgment is a subjective thought process, and the intuitions of the experienced should be given serious consideration, whether objectively justified or not.

Groups organized to run by consensus (at NOLS, a yes vote from the majority and agreement from all concerned to go along with the choice) offer both challenges and opportunities. This group decision-making can be a lengthy, time-consuming process, but consensus generally produces a fuller commitment to the group's goals than any other form of group management because all members state that they can at least live with the decision.

A leader may also choose to delegate decisions to other members of the group or to the group as a whole. The leader, however, must always be ready to step in if safety is being compromised.

A thoughtful leader varies his or her leadership style based on the circumstances. But in the end, how your group is organized is not nearly as important as how your group supports decisions with appropriate actions. Active "followership" is a part of all successful trips. All group members can show leadership, in fact, by being positive followers: seeking clarity, giving input tactfully, respecting the plan, helping out, and working for the betterment of the group.

Personal Leadership Skills

Basic social skills are the heart and soul of personal leadership skills. Without a solid, working relationship with the people being led, theories of leadership are no more than words. There are seven skill principles associated with leadership at NOLS:

1. *Competence.* Leaders must be proficient not only in technical skills, such as backcountry travel and construction of snow shelters, but also in group management skills. Leaders do not necessarily have to be the best in either area, but they must be able to perform competently in both areas.
2. *Self-Awareness.* Good leaders know themselves. They understand their limitations and needs, admit their mis-

takes, know when to seek feedback from others, and work continually to deepen self-knowledge. They are clear in their own minds and with others about their own values and goals.

3. *Judgment and Decision-Making.* Winter offers extreme cold, winds of ice-hard intensity, and the possibility of adverse snow conditions. The group may need to decide quickly whether to turn back from a peak or forge ahead. Leaders are able to blend their knowledge, experience, character, and situational awareness to make wise choices in all circumstances.

4. *Tolerance for Adversity and Uncertainty.* Not every situation can be anticipated—the snow might fall more heavily, the wind might blow harder, some of the group's interpersonal relationships might fall apart. Leaders must be ready to face the challenge of hard work and uncertainty.

5. *Expedition Behavior.* Group members need to take care of not only themselves—both physically and psychologically—but also one another. A critical component of leadership is the ability to respect team members and their efforts. Good expedition behavior is a balance of teamwork, personal initiative, and responsibility. Personal energy expended in the form of honesty, politeness, or helpfulness can add much to the success of a trip: Carry a little extra gear. Break a little more trail. Dig a little extra snow. Show the group, and yourself, that you're willing to do more than your share to help the team.

6. *Communication.* Leaders must have good communication skills. They need the courage to say what they think, feel, and want, and they need to listen to others' viewpoints. They need to provide clear, useful, and timely information and feedback. They need to be able to nip conflicts in the bud, confront problems head-on, and defuse tense situations (when appropriate, with humor). Leaders' most effective communication tool,

however, may be role-modeling: setting a good example by crawling out of an ice-encrusted sleeping bag to light the stove, consuming water at a disciplined rate, adjusting layers of clothing, stopping to warm a cold foot.

7. *Vision and Action.* Keeping the group focused on its goals—skiing a route, learning to build and live in snow shelters, staying healthy on the trail—is the leader's responsibility. Leaders help the group forge a vision and clarify a plan and then discipline the team to implement that plan with high energy and a can-do attitude.

Leadership in Extreme Situations

Winter creates additional stresses for individuals and an expedition. Factors such as the depth of the cold and the hard work of moving through snow add to the pressure put on leaders, who must keep the group together and moving toward its goals.

Some people fall apart emotionally when stresses are extreme; others ignore stress emotionally but still deal with it rationally. Those who fall apart lose their ability to think clearly. Crying, for instance, is not an example of "losing it," but crying and becoming helpless is. To take another example, when arguments arise over inane matters, the stress not only distracts the group but can lead to muscular tension, which burns calories, decreases coordination, and negatively impacts performance, increasing the chance of injury.

Leaders need to minimize their emotional reactions to stressful situations: Take a few deep breaths. Take nothing personally. Don't assume anything—ask for clarity. Think before you speak. Act appropriately and in the interests of the health and safety of the group.

NOLS TIP

Leave an Itinerary

Never leave home without providing a responsible person with your itineray so that, if necessary, he or she knows when and how to initiate a search for you. Details should include who is with you, where you are going (exactly), what you have with you, and when you plan to be back.

Chapter 2

Winter Clothing

Winter, with all its beauty and wonder, is cold. This fact must remain paramount in the minds of those who venture out in it. One's goal is not to endure but to thrive—to be safe, healthy, and highly functional. To that end, what to wear—and what to carry (see chapter 3)—is of the utmost importance.

HUMAN THERMOREGULATION

Let's start with the fundamentals of human thermodynamics—body heat gain versus body heat loss—and how that relates to what you wear. There are two major internal sources of heat. Even as you sit quietly reading this book, you are making heat via basal metabolism, the energy necessary to sustain life. When you get up and move around, a second heat source kicks in—exercise metabolism. Strenuous exercise metabolism can produce fifteen to eighteen times as much heat as basal metabolism, depending on your level of fitness. When you're outdoors in the cold, exercise is your major source of heat gain. You can also absorb some heat from external sources, such as the sun or a fire. You end up, after all heat production is totaled, with far more heat than you need, and if you couldn't shed the excess, you would literally cook in your own juices.

MECHANISMS OF Heat Loss

Human heat is lost in four ways: conduction, radiation, convection, and evaporation. Conduction, heat lost through direct contact with something cooler, can suck heat rapidly from exposed body parts and slowly from poorly insulated body parts. Radiation is energy lost directly from the skin surface; as the air cools down around you, radiative heat loss from a poorly insulated body may be substantial. Convection is heat lost through the movement of air—or water, if you fall into an icy lake—around your body. In wind, convective heat loss from exposed body parts is fast and furious, but even just walking causes some heat loss via convection. These three sources of heat loss can be greatly reduced, even stopped, with adequately insulated clothing.

The fourth source of heat loss—evaporation, or the vaporization of water from skin—is the primary method of human heat loss in most circumstances. As your skin heats up, pores dilate and sweat floods out. Evaporation of sweat, or of water from other sources, cools your skin; heat is drawn from the blood near the body's surface, and the cooler blood circulates to the inside. That's a healthy thing in extreme heat, but it can be a killer in the cold. Because a wet surface can lose heat an astounding twenty-five times faster than a dry surface, to prevent heat loss in winter you must stay not only warm but also dry.

> **WET COLD VERSUS DRY COLD**
>
> Air feels colder in wet environmental conditions. Humid (wet) air, which is more likely in maritime climates, doesn't conduct heat any faster than dry air does, but it definitely *feels* like it does. More important, wet conditions make it substantially more difficult to keep your insulation dry and, therefore, functioning at maximal efficiency. When it's both cold and humid, you need to take special care to stay dry.

When the environment is not a threat, your thermoregulatory system balances heat production and heat loss to keep you at about 98.6 degrees F (37 degrees C). You seldom have to think about it. In the cold, however, thoughtful planning and appropriate dress—and behavior—are essential to managing thermoregulation.

BASIC CLOTHING PRINCIPLES

Clothing lies between you and the frigid outdoors. It is your most immediate and intimate shelter. You may choose your everyday clothing based on how it makes you look, but when you're dressing for winter activities, your primary considerations should be (1) how well your garments trap body heat, and (2) how well they prevent vapor from condensing.

Clothing must insulate you, in a strictly physiological sense, from the environment. Its ability to insulate is directly related to the thickness of the "dead air" space (i.e., enclosed space that prevents air movement) it maintains around you. The dead air is warmed by your body heat, and since it can't move, it keeps the heat near you. There is really no such thing

THE DEW POINT

The temperature at which vapor condenses into liquid is called the dew point. When the air temperature rises, the dew point rises, and your clothing will retain more moisture. Then, as both the air temperature and the dew point decrease, the retained vapor in your clothing becomes liquid and freezes. Moisture frozen on the outside of clothing can be easily and harmlessly brushed off, but moisture frozen on the inside of clothing requires long and tedious drying to remove. Keep the dew point working in your favor by layering.

as "warm clothing." You provide the warmth, and if your clothing insulates well enough, you stay warm.

Your winter wardrobe must also provide protection from wind and precipitation. But at the same time, winter clothing must be constructed of materials that allow you to stay as dry as possible from the sweat you'll produce, and it must be worn in a manner that eliminates as much sweating as possible. Most of the sweat you produce should pass through your clothing before it freezes, allowing it to evaporate with little accumulation.

BASIC CLOTHING MATERIALS

Despite the plethora of clothing available to choose from, you actually have only three materials that are acceptable for winter use: wool, synthetics, and down.

Wool, once the "clothing" of some well-insulated animal, does an excellent job of trapping air between its crimped fibers. Depending on its thickness and the way it is woven, wool cloth may be more than 75% air, making it a great insulator. Amazingly, wool even retains its ability to insulate when wet. Wool absorbs water into its fibers, leaving the wearer with little of the negative thermoregulatory effects of being wet. Because of this, however, it can also become extremely heavy. In addition, it releases moisture slowly, taking a long time to dry. Tightly woven wool also provides a high level of windproofing.

Wool can be relatively inexpensive if you shop surplus stores, and it can be comfortable (non-itchy) if you don't mind paying the price for products manufactured in some modern, mysterious way that removes the itchiness. Wool can function well as a base layer and in middle layers (see the section on layering beginning on page 16), but it is not the best choice as an outer layer in precipitation. Also, wool doesn't compact well, so it can require quite a bit of pack room.

Synthetic materials (plastics) are spun into fibers and woven into garments to make them feel soft and comfortable against your skin. The ability of synthetics to insulate is comparable to that of wool, depending, again, on their thickness, the way they are woven, and the type of plastic used—polyester is warmer than polyethylene, which is warmer than nylon. Synthetics retain much of their insulation value when wet, but they hold less moisture than wool and aren't as heat-retentive when wet. However, because the fibers of synthetic materials do not absorb water, they dry much more quickly. The moisture moves—"wicks"—away from a warm body along the fibers of the material. Synthetics are generally more lightweight than wool and take up less space in your pack. They make excellent base layers (sold as undergarments in various thicknesses,) middle layers (usually sold as "pile" or "fleece"), and outer layers.

Tightly woven synthetic cloth, the kind used in outer garments, blocks wind and, if coated, keeps precipitation out. Pile and fleece, however, do next to nothing to stop a hard wind. Some brands, to compensate, incorporate a windproof layer in the design. But keep in mind that windproof fleece doesn't keep out much precipitation; you'll still need a shell if there is any chance of rain or snow (and there is almost always a chance). And when you add a water-resistant shell over windproof fleece, the garment's ability to transport moisture is inhibited. That inhibition can be positive or negative, depending on variables such as the amount of precipitation and your level of exercise.

Down, composed of the small inner feathers of certain birds, offers a great amount of dead air space without much weight. It also compresses into a small space. Down-filled gar-

VAPOR BARRIERS

Vapor barriers include any clothing—or even a plastic bag, in a pinch—that allows no water to pass through. Since this prevents perspiration from passing through, the sweat stays near the skin. Over time, the humidity level near the skin rises to the point where sweating slows or perhaps even stops. A vapor barrier, therefore, may slow the loss of body fluid and reduce evaporative heat loss. Vapor barriers are more comfortable when they are not directly in contact with skin. For instance, you should wear a thin liner sock between your foot and a vapor barrier. Vapor barriers' utility varies with the individual. Some people simply don't feel comfortable in a vapor barrier; they feel "clammy." In addition, individuals perspire at different rates. A person who sweats heavily may "fill" a vapor barrier sock to the point where the moisture actually increases heat loss. If you like the idea of vapor barriers, you'll have to experiment to see if they work for you.

ments provide excellent insulation; in fact, only in the most extreme cold would you be comfortable wearing down while exercising.

Down absorbs water readily and aggressively and takes a very long time to dry; once wet, it practically loses its ability to insulate. Down-filled garments, though certainly useful (such as when you're sitting around camp on a frozen night), require a lot of care compared with other garments and typically come with a large price tag. Down-filled clothing seldom has a place in an active layering system—other than an occasional vest.

LAYERING

As your environment and level of activity change, so will your clothing needs. This means you will need to be adjusting clothing layers carefully when winter camping. The principle of layering is common knowledge: an outer layer over middle layers over a base layer. The base layer provides little insulation, but, if made out of the proper material (see page 18) it will transport moisture toward the outside, keeping you relatively dry at skin level. Middle layers provide the insulation and ideally keep moving moisture toward the outside. In certain conditions, the outermost middle layer also serves as the outer layer. A true outer layer, sometimes called a shell, serves primarily to protect you from wind and precipitation. Some shell materials also keep moisture moving toward the outside. When you purchase articles of clothing to be worn in layers, you need to try them on all at once to make sure the outer layers are big enough. Tight-fitting clothing reduces the dead air space and thus the insulation.

The greatest value of layering, however, is not in the layers themselves but in the ability to add and remove them. Under normal conditions, how much you sweat is determined by skin temperature: cooler skin means less sweat. Even in extremes of cold, however, you may become overheated due to exertion, and a too-late decision to remove a layer can result in a body drenched in sweat. Conversely, a too-late decision to add a layer can result in a loss of body heat. With a little experience, you can become an expert in layering—shedding or ventilating a layer before heating up, and adding a layer before cooling off. It is a process that has to happen regularly in the cold outdoors.

Those new to winter travel might imagine themselves bulked out in so much clothing that they can't move. This is not necessarily so. The evolution of "technical" clothing allows you to cover up with fabrics that stretch but still insulate, and other materials that insulate without being thick. With a bit of smart shopping, your winter wardrobe can include a layering system to meet your specific needs without a lot of bulk. And keep in mind that some people simply stay warmer than others and require fewer or lighter layers. Your pack should contain all you might need, but not a clothes rack from the local outdoor store. In this case, experimentation is the answer. And the wise winter traveler stays close to the car or carries a few extra layers during the experimentation phase.

NOLS TIP

Wear Your Sleeping Bag

If you feel the need for an extra layer, wear your sleeping bag like a cloak. It will trap your body heat and be warmer when you're ready to crawl into it at bedtime.

BASE LAYER : "LONG UNDERWEAR" or LIGHT BASE LAYER
WICKS MOISTURE AWAY FROM YOUR BODY

Base Layers

Base layers, commonly referred to as "long underwear," are available in lightweight, middleweight, or heavyweight (also called expedition-weight), depending on the season. Shirts come in short-sleeve and long-sleeve versions, and they are available with crew necks, turtlenecks, and zip turtlenecks. For winter camping, a middleweight long-sleeve top and bottom will usually do the job. Save the expedition-weight base layers for true extremes of cold like those found in the polar regions and at high altitudes. Some people prefer to pack a lightweight and a heavyweight top and bottom, allowing more options in layering. A zip turtle-neck top with a partial front zipper offers the best control over ventilation and thus provides another way to regulate temperature. The base layer must actively wick moisture away from your skin, making synthetics the best choice in material. Synthetic base layers all stretch to some degree, allowing them to do their job without adding much bulk.

> **N O L S   T I P**
>
> **Use Zipper Pulls**
>
> *Little pieces of cloth or cord that attach to zippers make them easier to manage, especially with cold hands or hands encased in gloves or mittens.*

Since base layers are effectively underwear, you may not need briefs or other "conventional" undergarments. Should you want them anyway, however, make sure they're not cotton, or they'll defeat your attempts to stay dry at skin level.

Middle Layers

The middle layers of your clothing system, the insulating layers, can take the form of jackets, sweaters, pullovers, or vests on top, and pants on the bottom. When discussing middle layers, the terms "jacket" and "sweater" are sometimes used interchangeably, but in general jackets (such as the Mountain Hardwear Windstopper Jacket) are multi-feature garments with large pockets, whereas sweaters (such as the Columbia Sportswear Steens Mountain Sweater) are simpler and are often without pockets. If you get cold easily, jackets are also available with insulation. Whatever you choose, make sure it has a full front zipper, which makes ventilation easier than with pullovers. For additional warmth, a zippered vest provides an excellent midlayer without too much bulk and with little restriction of movement.

Variety is the operative word when it comes to midlayer design features, which include hoods, pockets, zippers, and patches of stretchy material. You'll also find great differences in the cost of middle layers, depending partly on the material, but probably more on the number of design features. What

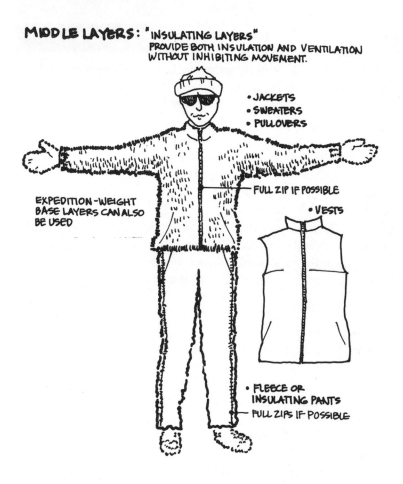

MIDDLE LAYERS: "INSULATING LAYERS"
PROVIDE BOTH INSULATION AND VENTILATION
WITHOUT INHIBITING MOVEMENT.

• JACKETS
• SWEATERS
• PULLOVERS

EXPEDITION-WEIGHT
BASE LAYERS CAN ALSO
BE USED

FULL ZIP IF POSSIBLE

• VESTS

• FLEECE OR
INSULATING PANTS
FULL ZIPS IF POSSIBLE

you choose will vary according to how warm you need to feel and how many features you desire or can afford. When you make your choice, consider the ease with which you can add or remove the layer; one pants option most people find appealing is full or partial leg zippers to aid in dressing and undressing. There are also gender-specific midlayer pants available that offer an additional zipper to make it easier for women to urinate.

As mentioned earlier, expedition-weight undergarments can be used as middle layers in most conditions.

Outer Layers

Lightweight wind shells for your upper body, such as the Mountain Hardwear Phantom, weigh only a few ounces and squeeze down to the size of an average fist. They breathe well enough for you to wear during strenuous exercise on a windy day. Because they are light and typically fit snugly, you can even add a layer of fleece over the shell if you feel your body heat escaping too rapidly. Although they might stand up to light precipitation, the primary purpose of wind shells is to repel wind.

BREATHABILITY

"Breathability" refers to a material's capacity to allow moisture on the inside to escape while repelling moisture from the outside. For the winter traveler, breathable garments are an excellent choice. Snow can't get in, but sweat can get out. The breathability of specific materials is highly variable. The more waterproof a material is, the less breathable it is. In the end, you are left to experiment until you find a garment that works best for you. And no matter how breathable a garment is, you can still sweat profusely if you are overinsulated beneath it.

Soft shells, such as the Mountain Hardwear Synchro, block wind and repel a steady fall of precipitation while maintaining a high degree of breathability, but they are heavier than wind shells and don't compress nearly as well into small spaces in your pack. When the temperature ranges from uncomfortably chilly to mighty cold, and when the precipitation falls lightly to moderately, a soft shell is an excellent choice. Many different manufacturers offer soft shells for the upper and lower body, and their ability to breathe and to repel moisture varies widely.

Waterproof/breathable shells are windproof as well as waterproof, but despite the name, these shells don't breathe as well as lightweight wind shells and soft shells. You can sacrifice some breathability when less water is getting in in the first place. Many manufacturers offer these shells with features designed to aid ventilation:

NOLS TIP

Minimize Insulation

When traveling, wear as little insulation as possible under an outer shell to keep the water vapor you produce to a minimum.

OUTER LAYER: "SHELL", WINDPROOF AND/OR WATERPROOF
FURTHER INSULATES WHILE PROTECTING FROM
WIND and PRECIPITATION

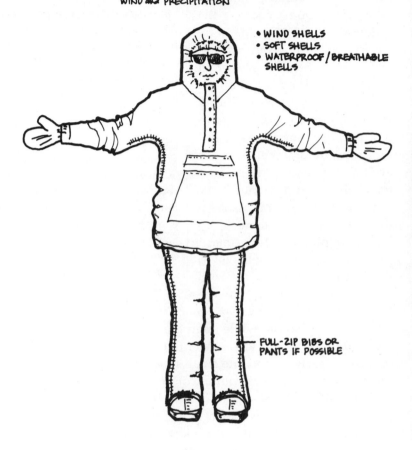

- WIND SHELLS
- SOFT SHELLS
- WATERPROOF / BREATHABLE SHELLS

FULL-ZIP BIBS OR
PANTS IF POSSIBLE

zippered armpits, mesh-lined pockets, or highly breathable material in areas that need venting. For extremes of cold, waterproof/breathable upper-body shells, with hoods full enough to keep snow and wind off your face, are usually the best bet. For your lower body, go with bibs such as the North Face Steep Tech Pants. Bibs rise up high on your torso, sometimes almost to your armpits, with straps that go over your shoulders. They keep snow out of your clothing much better

23

CLOTHING CARE TIPS

1. Keep your clothing clean, according to the manufacturer's instructions. Dirt not only shortens the life of technical clothing but also reduces the breathability of fabrics and speeds the deterioration of water-repellent coatings. And the salt in sweat can collect in synthetic base layers and will begin to irritate your skin if it isn't washed out occasionally.
2. Waterproof/breathable materials, although they work best when clean, can be harmed by overwashing, which will eventually wear off the waterproof coating. Limit the laundering of these garments to once or twice a year. Most of these materials can withstand twenty or so appropriate washings without significant harm.
3. Wash down-filled garments only when absolutely necessary, and always use a soap made especially for down. Most detergents strip the protective oils off down feathers. Down is also notoriously difficult to dry, a process that often causes it to clump.
4. Some clothing deteriorates in the heat of a dryer. In most cases, you're better off hanging technical clothing indoors to dry. Some water-repellent coatings, however, are actually enhanced by dryer heat. Check with the manufacturer.
5. Do not dry synthetics near open flames, because they might melt.
6. Retire technical clothing when you see layers peeling off or seams separating.
7. If your garment falls apart sooner than expected, contact the manufacturer. Most manufacturers will repair or replace faulty clothing that fails to meet their claims.

than pants do. Side zippers add greatly to ease of use with either bibs or pants.

In certain situations, such as a late-spring ski tour with the possibility of heavy rain, you may opt for a shell that is completely waterproof and has zero breathability. In this case, look for a synthetic outer layer with an interior coating that allows no moisture in or out.

HEADGEAR

If your feet are cold, put on a hat—an old maxim, and essentially a true one. The brain, the control center of the human

HEADWEAR

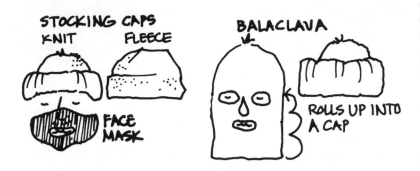

body, will sacrifice less critical body parts to save itself. It will, in other words, attempt to maintain adequate blood flow to the head, no matter what. Thus, an uncovered head can cause a large amount of heat to be lost to the environment.

There are numerous headgear options to consider, and the well-prepared winter traveler carries more than one type. If you're wearing a garment with a hood, you have an immediate covering for your head. An earband, preferably made from a windproof fabric, may be all you need when you're exercising hard and the temperature is not too low. A lightweight wool or synthetic stocking cap is more appropriate when the temperature drops below moderate and you're still working hard. For periods of low to no activity, you'll want a thicker stocking cap, or perhaps a fleece-lined hat with earflaps—you can turn the flaps up or down, depending on how cold you feel. When the temperature plummets, you'll probably want a very thick stocking cap or a balaclava to cover your head, your neck, and most of your face. A balaclava can be rolled up into a stocking cap when you don't feel the need for face coverage.

In extremes of cold (below 0° F.), especially with a wind blowing, you should be able to cover your face as well as the rest of your head. You can suffer frostbite to your face—nose, cheeks, and lips—in a relatively brief period of time. Covering bare skin is generally a more effective way to trap body heat than adding a layer. If you notice the cold stinging your nose, it's time to cover up. Without a balaclava, or even with one, a facemask is a healthy choice, and one made of neoprene or a similar material usually works best, because condensation from breathing will form little or no ice on the outside of the mask. When neither a balaclava nor a facemask is available, a scarf can be tied around your face.

Your eyes require protection from extreme cold, as well as protection from ultraviolet light (see chapter 8). Deep cold and windblown ice particles can damage your eyes and actually freeze your eyelids shut. Sunglasses should wrap around your eyes to provide full coverage. Glacier glasses have shields at the corners of the eyes to provide protection from the sides; the downside of glacier glasses is the loss of peripheral vision, a problem that nags at some winter travelers but doesn't bother others. Goggles, such as those worn by alpine skiers, may be necessary when it's terribly cold and windy. With any enclosed glasses, the problem of fogging increases when you work up a sweat, and anti-fog products may be worthy of consideration.

HANDWEAR

Even with your torso, arms, legs, and head well cared for in terms of clothing, your fingers can still freeze without special consideration. Fingers are not only small but also relatively far from the warmth of the body's core. They get cold easily and are often difficult to warm up. Mittens are better for maintaining warmth, since they allow the fingers to share their heat, but gloves give you greater dexterity. To counter their respective drawbacks, there are gloves available that provide a great deal of insulation, and some mittens have flip-tops that allow you to expose your fingers. You

NOLS TIP

Keep Your Gloves Warm

When you remove your gloves, immediately put them in a pocket to keep them warm and dry. Never set them in the snow.

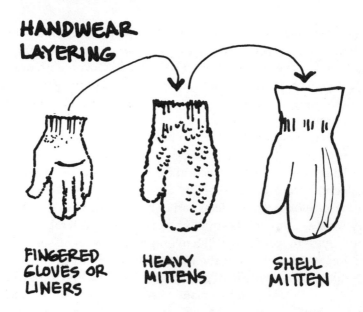

HANDWEAR LAYERING

FINGERED GLOVES OR LINERS

HEAVY MITTENS

SHELL MITTEN

can also wear light gloves inside of bulky mittens and remove the mittens for short periods when you need your fingers. In mild to moderate cold, well-insulated gloves may be enough. In severe cold, you'll want heavy mittens. In the most extreme cold, you'll do best with a layering system for your hands: a liner glove inside a thick mitten inside a waterproof/breathable shell mitten. When in doubt, go with the layering system. It doesn't weigh a lot, and you'll be ready for anything winter throws at you.

FOOTWEAR

Your feet, especially your toes, tend to suffer first and foremost from the cold, being farthest from the body's core. To avoid sacrificing them to the flesh-hungry gods of winter, choose your boots and socks carefully. In addition to temperature, consider your mode of travel—skiing, snowshoeing, mountaineering—when picking appropriate footwear. Even if you're trying to reduce the cost of getting set up for winter camping, do not skimp here.

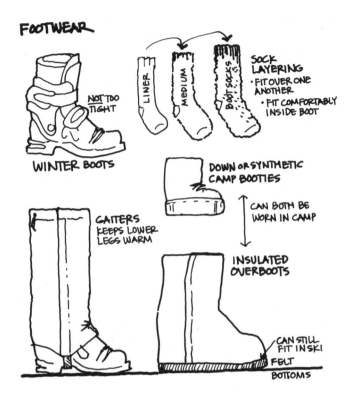

FOOTWEAR

NOT TOO TIGHT

WINTER BOOTS

LINER

MEDIUM

BOOT SOCKS

SOCK LAYERING
• FIT OVER ONE ANOTHER
  • FIT COMFORTABLY INSIDE BOOT

DOWN OR SYNTHETIC CAMP BOOTIES

CAN BOTH BE WORN IN CAMP

GAITERS KEEPS LOWER LEGS WARM

INSULATED OVERBOOTS

CAN STILL FIT IN SKI

FELT BOTTOMS

Boots

It is only common sense that boots worn in winter should, in fact, be winter boots. Winter boots are generally distinguished from regular boots by being insulated and large enough to accommodate thicker socks. Putting on an extra pair of socks and stuffing your feet into thin boots is asking for discomfort and disaster, as the tighter fit will reduce heat-bearing circulation and dead air.

Two important characteristics to look for in winter boots are their resistance to the elements and their ability to hold in body heat. Since you can almost always expect to get your boots wet, choose boots that are either waterproof or made from materials to which you can apply a waterproofing product. Breathable boots will minimize sweating, and boots with waterproof/breathable liners are available. Some winter

---

TIPS FOR BUYING BOOTS

All boots are built around a "last," an ideal form to which the boot is fit. Only by trying on many different models and walking around in them can you determine whether a specific boot fits you. Boot fit is essential for keeping your feet warm.

1. Shop later in the day, because your feet tend to swell a bit during normal activities.
2. Try on the boots with the socks you intend to wear while traveling in winter.
3. Be sure the laces are snug enough to hold your heel in place. Your heel should have little space for lateral movement and a minimum of up-and-down movement. At the ball of your foot, right at the base of your toes, there should be contact with the sides of the boot—a supportive pressure, not a cramped feeling. Along the arch of your foot, you should feel gentle contact with the boot. From the ball forward, there should be decreasing contact, and your toes should be able to wiggle freely.
4. Test the fit by pressing your booted foot firmly against a wall, checking to see if the contact points remain relatively constant and if the toes stay free.
5. Don't overtighten the boots; you should still be able to loosen or tighten the laces. (You may want to tighten the laces for steep downhill trails and loosen them for steep uphill routes.)
6. Pay attention to the pressure of the boot's cuff on your ankle or shin. It should not be uncomfortable when you walk.

---

boots, like sleeping bags, have a manufacturer's rating based on the lowest temperature at which they will protect your feet. Unfortunately, you can't know for sure until you've hiked around in them. It is far more important that the boots be well insulated. Look for a thick sole to protect your feet from the icy ground and a tread that provides traction on snow and ice. And if you plan to wear the boots with snowshoes, make sure, before buying, that the boots fit the bindings of the snowshoes. Although this is seldom a problem, it's best to know for sure.

Not surprisingly, there are a number of different types of winter footwear available, and they often work best in combination:

Insulated, or Pack, Boots. Several manufacturers offer boots insulated against extreme cold with rubber bottoms, leather uppers, and dense wool felt liners. They hold in a lot of body heat, but once the liners get wet, they dry slowly. Experienced winter travelers often substitute synthetic liners, which dry faster. These boots also fit more loosely than stiffer boots, and some people don't like the way their feet slap around inside. They do, however, work well with snowshoes.

Mountaineering Boots. These consist of rigid outer boots with wool felt or closed-cell foam inner boots. The outer boots are often plastic, but heavy leather mountaineering boots are available. They hold body heat well, the foam liners dry quickly, and the boots work well with crampons and many ski bindings.

Ski Touring Boots. These are specialized boots with insulation, waterproofing or a high level of water resistance, and breathability, as well as enough support and flexibility to allow the motions of skiing. At one time, the uppers were made exclusively of leather, but many of these boots are now made of synthetic materials.

Insulated Overboots. Like a gaiter (see page 30), these can be worn with mountaineering boots or ski touring boots for added insulation. They can also be worn alone as camp overboots.

Mukluks. One-piece moccasins that reach to just below the knee, mukluks have a thick, removable lining (often wool felt). Immensely flexible and highly breathable, they are very comfortable but difficult to waterproof. Therefore, they are not the best choice when it's wet and cold rather than dry and cold. Most people prefer more support than mukluks provide.

Camp Booties. These are basically fat socks filled with a synthetic fiber or down. They are very nice for added foot insulation while lounging in the tent or sleeping.

Camp Overboots. These are shells with an insulated bottom. They can be worn with dry socks or booties for a walk to the pee-tree or for doing light camp chores.

BOOT CARE TIPS
---

1. Clean your boots with a stiff brush after every trip.
2. Dry your boots after every trip. Avoid drying boots in direct sunlight or near a high heat source. Remove the insole to ensure that it dries well. A wad of newspaper stuffed inside each boot for a few hours will absorb moisture.
3. Treat your leather boots with a waterproofing product at the start of each winter and any time they begin to look dried out.
4. Store your boots in a dry, relatively warm place.

Once you have chosen a pair of boots, don't forget the all-important break-in time—the time required for the boots to adapt to your personal flex patterns. For the first week, wear the boots around the house or on short walks. By the end of the first week, you should be able to wear the boots comfortably all day, but keep wearing them around town for a second week before hitting the snowy trail under a pack.

Socks

Feet are usually warmest in a layered sock system in which thin synthetic liner socks wick moisture into one or two pairs of thicker outer socks. Be sure that the outer socks are big enough to fit over the inner socks without compromising insulation and circulation. You may also need to alter your sock system depending on your boots. Wool (especially merino wool) makes a great outer sock, but synthetics and wool-synthetic blends are also fine choices. Dry feet are an absolute necessity, and carrying at least three sock systems is recommended. You'll also want to keep a dry pair for the luxury of cozy feet during those long nights in the sleeping bag.

Gaiters

Gaiters are leg coverings that reach from your instep to your lower leg, keeping snow out of your boots and moisture away from your leg and providing insulation. They come in various sizes, but for winter, choose a pair that reaches to just below

---

BASIC WINTER CLOTHING CHECKLIST

☐ Base layers
  ☐ Lightweight long-sleeve zip turtleneck
  ☐ Heavyweight long-sleeve zip turtleneck
  ☐ Lightweight pants
  ☐ Heavyweight pants (in extreme cold)
☐ Middle layers
  ☐ Pile sweater
  ☐ Pile vest
  ☐ Pile pants with side zipper
☐ Outer layers
  ☐ Waterproof/breathable parka with full hood
  ☐ Waterproof/breathable bibs
☐ Stocking cap
☐ Balaclava
☐ Lightweight gloves
☐ Wool mittens
☐ Shell mittens
☐ Ski boots
☐ Camp booties
☐ Wool socks (3 pairs)
☐ Liner socks (3 pairs)
☐ Gaiters

---

your knees. Also, select a pair that closes in front with a zipper or hook-and-loop strips (such as Velcro) and has a strap that wraps from the bottom of the gaiter under the arch of your boot, to keep them from riding up when you step down into snow. They should at least be water-resistant—preferably waterproof—and, ideally, they should breathe.

Chapter 3

Winter Gear

When it comes to choosing gear for winter, you are faced with many options. And by the time you finish reading this sentence, the choices will have multiplied. You could leave the decision to someone else, but that's not the best way to approach the outdoors in winter (or life). With that in mind, this chapter provides guidelines to help you generate a list of the basic things you'll need, as well as information to help you make educated choices about which specific items to carry.

SKIS AND ACCESSORIES
Not everyone travels on skis in winter, but there are good reasons for doing so. When the white stuff lies deep enough for you to sink into it, you want to ride on top as easily and smoothly and, sometimes, as quickly as possible. With skis you can slide over flat and rolling terrain, climb hills, and—the most fun of all—glide back down. And once you get the hang of it, skiing takes less energy than any other method of snow travel, so you arrive less tired.

Skiing on a winter camping trip differs from skiing on the manicured slopes and groomed trails of civilization. For one thing, the condition of the snow can vary remarkably over a relatively short distance. Deep and soft snow may become

firm and icy or wet and slushy, or you may find yourself skiing over a crust that collapses periodically under your weight.
With a group of skiers, you might find yourself enjoying the
tracks of those ahead or laboring to break a trail. In other
words, you need to be ready for anything and have gear that
can handle a wide range of conditions.

Skis

To begin with, you probably won't be wearing alpine skis—
the ones under your feet at ski resorts—although the finan-
cially challenged could get by on old alpine skis if they are
flexible enough. In a perfect snowy world, you'll be wearing
what are known as backcountry skis. And here, of course, you
have some choices.

Skinny skis are lighter, usually longer, and always faster
on the flats, but they don't float as well as fat skis do in deep
stuff. Fatter skis break a trail more easily and are easier to
turn. In general, a shorter, fatter ski is a better all-around
choice, especially if this will be your first ski trip into the wild
country. The salesperson can give you advice on how long
your skis should be, based on your height and weight. But
going as lightweight as possible is advised, since you may be
carrying your skis from time to time. Skis are wider at the tip
and tail than in the middle, and this difference is called the

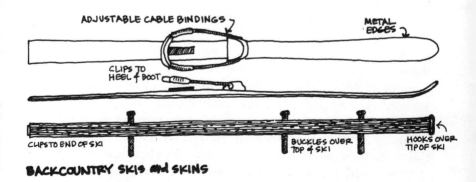

BACKCOUNTRY SKIS AND SKINS

SNOWSHOE VERSUS SKI

The basic snowshoe has served the same purpose for centuries: it distributes your weight over a larger area, allowing you to walk through snow without sinking in. But snowshoe technology has changed dramatically in recent times. Improvements include more secure, easier-to-manage bindings and lighter, stronger materials. There have also been significant cost increases to match the higher quality. Still, a great snowshoe costs less than a great ski. How much you pay depends on how much shoe you want, which depends on what you plan to do—short trips with a light pack, or long expeditions under a heavy load. Other advantages are that it is easier to learn to snowshoe than to ski (and you fall less often), and snowshoes are easier to handle on narrow, twisting trails and steep ascents. A fine set of snowshoes can grip the snow better than skis can, especially if the bindings have teeth where the shoe meets the snow. They weigh less than skis, and they make better improvised shovels than skis do.

Nonetheless, NOLS uses skis on winter camping trips for a number of reasons. Apart from their purely educational role in the NOLS curriculum (there is, quite simply, more to learn about skis than snowshoes), skis are much faster when a basic level of competence is reached—you go farther and see more. And, most importantly in some minds, skis are just more fun to use. For more information on travelling with snowshoes, we recommend *Snowshoeing: From Novice to Master, Fifth Edition* by Gene Prater.

sidecut. The greater the sidecut, the faster a ski will turn. Conversely, skis with less sidecut run a straighter line on flats.

The skis should be more flexible than the ones you wear in lift lines, allowing the tips to ride up in soft snow instead of burying themselves below the surface. Skis with metal edges hold an edge better on hard surfaces, such as ice or windslab, and the edge is more durable.

Another choice is between waxable and waxless skis. "Waxless" is a somewhat misleading term, however, because all skis require some waxing. The types are differentiated by whether wax must be applied to the kick zone, the middle part of the ski where traction is either gained or lost. Waxable skis grip better for more traction and faster travel, if you've waxed them appropriately for the conditions—not always an easy undertaking. And the wax has to be reapplied, sometimes more than once a day, so you have to carry a wax kit. Waxless skis have some type of a fish-scale pattern on the bottom for traction. They work well enough in most conditions and their maintenance is less time-intensive, but they don't glide as well. For more information on waxing, see page 64.

Bindings

Bindings are designed to hold your skis to your boots. A three-pin binding attaches the boot firmly at the toe only. This is simple and light, but the binding can break under the pressure of hard skiing with heavy loads, and the pinholes easily clog with ice on expeditions. A cable binding attaches the boot at the toe firmly and has a cable that wraps around the heel. This type stands up to much more abuse and is probably a better choice for most backcountry skiers. There are also combination bindings with three pins and a cable. On the upside, these bindings hold your boots very securely, but on the downside, they release much less easily—a problem if you fall a lot on steep terrain or find yourself caught in an avalanche. Both three-pin and cable bindings leave your heel entirely free. A third type of binding, the randonnee, allows you to either free your heels or bind them to your skis for extreme downhill routes. The randonnee can take a mountaineering boot—a plus—but on long hauls, it is generally considered less comfortable.

Make sure that the skis do not have what are known as safety straps. These will inhibit your ability to shed the skis quickly if an avalanche occurs.

Skins

Skins are long, thin pieces of synthetic material, such as nylon, attached to the bottom of your skis. (They were once made of sealskins, hence the name.) "Hairs" on the skin point backward, allowing you to push forward easily, but they catch and hold if the ski starts to slide backward. If you expect to encounter significant uphill terrain, you'll want skins. They work on both waxable and waxless skis, and they either glue on or strap on. Glue-on skins stick better for superior traction, and they glide more easily. However, they cost more and are more time-intensive to put on and care for (you may have to dry them from time to time on extended trips), and if the temperature dips, you might find yourself duct-taping your glue-on skins on. Strap-on skins are often chosen, especially on longer expeditions, because of their ease of use and maintenance. In either case, the skins need to fit the skis, so take your skis with you when you buy skins.

SKI POLES AND AVALANCHE PROBES

You'll want ski poles for winter travel, even if you're not skiing. They enhance balance, help ease the weight of a pack off your shoulders, and lessen the strain on your legs. Fixed-length poles, if they are long enough, are adequate. "Long enough" means that the poles come up to your armpits when they are held upright at your side. (For cranking hard turns on a downhill slope, however, you'll want skis that allow a comfortable grip with the tips on the ground and your arms bent at a right angle.) More expensive adjustable poles have one or two movable sections that allow you to lengthen the poles on flats and shorten them for steep ascents and descents. When fully collapsed, adjustable poles fit nicely under the straps of your pack.

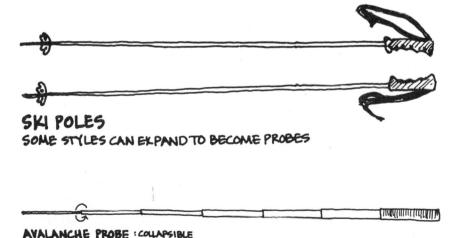

SKI POLES
SOME STYLES CAN EXPAND TO BECOME PROBES

AVALANCHE PROBE : COLLAPSIBLE

You can, of course, "adjust" the length of a pole by simply moving your hand off the grip and holding it at the length you want. One method is to take your hand out of the loop attached to the grip, stick your thumb through the loop, and grip the pole at the farthest extent of the loop. You can also wrap duct tape thickly around the pole to create a "grip" at a different spot. The duct tape grip should be added before leaving home, and it might come in handy in other ways if you happen to need a strip or two.

If you'll be traveling in avalanche terrain, you should have an avalanche probe. Some ski poles convert into probes, but most experienced winter travelers prefer a true avalanche probe. It's faster to use, and it tends to move through layers of snow better, reaching down twice as far as improvised probes. For ease of packing, probes break down into short lengths that are usually shock-corded together.

PACKS

If you've got a pack that works in summer, you've probably got a pack that works in winter. The most important consideration for a winter pack versus a summer pack is capacity. You need a pack that will hold all the additional supplies you need in winter. And if you don't own an internal frame pack, you should consider getting one: it keeps the load closer to your body, reducing the chance that you'll be thrown off balance when you're skiing. There are also pack design features that can make traveling in winter easier and more enjoyable.

A monster pack, something with 6,000 to 7,000-plus cubic inches of space, will undoubtedly hold as much as—or more than—you can carry. One bonus with large, well-made packs is a series of external compression straps that allow you to squeeze down the load for better balance if you don't fill all the space. Alternatively, you may be happy with a midrange pack, something with 4,000 to 5,000 cubic inches, especially if you are hauling some of your stuff in a sled or are considering trips of no more than a week. You may also want a smaller pack, with around 2,000 to 3,000 cubic inches, to use for day trips away from your base camp.

Few people would argue against a large pack for winter, but some advise against a pack with a lot of design features. The more additional straps and zippers it has, the more things there are that can freeze up, break off, or otherwise let you down. Extra features also mean extra cost. If you're committed to economy and simplicity, choose a large top-loading pack with few, if any, external features. External side or back pockets do let you organize your gear and clothing for quick access, but if you plan to carry your skis part of the time on your

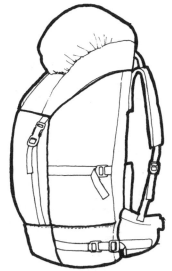

BASIC INTERNAL FRAME PACK

pack (if, for instance, you won't hit snow until you reach higher elevations), they can get in the way. Side zippers on a pack allow easy access to the gear inside without the addition of pockets. Another feature chosen by many winter travelers is a shovel pocket on the back of the pack, which can also be used for other things. Ice ax loops are common features on many packs, and, ideally, the ax should be held in place with a

---

PACK COMFORT

Winter travelers with a lot of miles under their hip belts have learned the importance of having a comfortable pack. That means buying a pack from a knowledgeable dealer who understands how to fit the pack to your body. The pack should be matched to your height and weight, shoulder width, and torso length. Higher-quality packs have an adjustable suspension system, and the initial adjustments should be made before you leave the store. As always, the final choice should be based not on what you are told but on how you feel. Choose comfort.

quick-release buckle on the upper end. You may also choose a pack with attachment straps for ski poles. External side compression straps (mentioned earlier) make excellent ski and ski pole attachment straps if they have quick-release buckles. Consider also that you'll want easy access to drinking water without removing your pack. Bottle pockets are light and relatively inexpensive features, but they don't offer the insulation of the main compartment of the pack, so freezing is more likely. Extra features, of course, also add extra weight, and there's no good reason to burden yourself with more than you need. But even a highly technical winter pack weighs no more than three or four pounds empty, and cutting a few ounces at the expense of accessibility and comfort may not be wise. In the end, you'll choose design features based on personal preference more than anything else—except, perhaps, your bank account.

SLEDS

Small sleds, sometimes known as pulks, are often used by skiers on extended winter trips. They allow you to take quite a bit of weight off your shoulders and pack it into a little "baggage compartment" that slides behind you—easily in the best conditions, arduously in the worst. Sleds are constructed of fiberglass, wood, or aluminum, but plastic sleds are almost always the best choice. Fiberglass and wood wear out, requiring resurfacing, and aluminum tends to ice up in some conditions. Plastic sleds are reliable and lightweight. The lightweight

SLED WITH DUFFEL BAG

aspect is important in terrain where you might have to carry the sled on your back for part of the day. And plastic sleds can be very inexpensive if, for instance, you choose a "toy" sled from the local we-have-it-all store and attach a rope for towing.

Rigid poles are essential for traverses and for maintaining control when going downhill. Runners also help on traverses in some snow conditions. If you expect hilly terrain, a high-end sled with a rigid harness system and runners such as a Mountainsmith is a great investment.

Some people prefer integral sled covers—fabric covers that attach to the side of the sled—to protect their gear. Another method is to fill a large duffel bag, one about the size of the sled's bottom. When the duffel is packed, it can be thrown on the sled and lashed on. Unlashed, the duffel can be hauled into a snow cave. Note that having a sled may tempt you to pack more stuff than you actually need—a temptation that is best resisted.

TENTS AND TARPS

When you reach a campsite, you'll be either setting up a tent or tarp or building a snow shelter. If you've opted for a tent or tarp, you've chosen the simpler and faster route to bedding down.

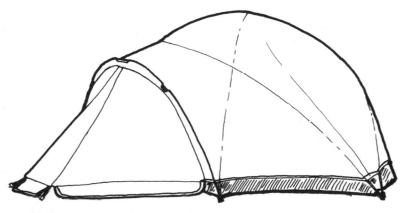

DOUBLE-WALL TENT WITH VESTIBULE

A winter tent, one that shelters a happy camper, must satisfy several requirements. Primarily, it needs to stand up to strong winds and heavy loads of snow. As a result, winter tents are heavier, being made of more solid fabric and less mesh, and use a greater number of poles for added strength. Winter tents are also larger than tents for other seasons, owing to the need to store gear inside. The tent should be well ventilated, allowing air movement to carry out the moisture exhaled by sleepers. If moisture collects on the inside of a tent, it can freeze, making the tent considerably heavier, or it may drip on the occupants. The desirable qualities in a winter tent tend to add substantially to the price as well as the weight.

Other specific features of a good winter tent are as follows:

- An adequate number of poles (generally, three to five). The more poles there are, the more stable the tent will be. The poles should be aluminum or carbon fiber. Fiberglass poles tend to break in extreme cold.
- Multiple reinforced points for stakes and stabilizing lines.
- Two doors for cross-ventilation, or at least vents that allow adequate ventilation. Ideally, the doors should have two-way zippers and a vestibule or hood that allows you to open them partway without letting snow in.
- At least one vestibule large enough to cook in and store some gear.
- Enough room to house people and at least some gear without anyone's sleeping bag touching the sides. Bags that touch the sides will get wet if moisture collects inside the tent.
- A profile that shrugs off high winds.
- A fly that reaches almost to the tent's bottom—tents with this feature are sometimes referred to as double-wall tents. Single-wall tents are quite a bit lighter and keep out the weather just as well, but despite modern

technology, they collect condensation more easily and never stay dry inside. Gore-tex tents won't breathe well enough to work in winter.

A tarp offers a few advantages over a tent: lighter weight, lower cost, and the versatility to become a dining fly outside of your snow shelter. A tarp can be a simple piece of nylon strung between trees, or it can resemble a fancy pyramid (such as the Black Diamond Megamid) held up by a center pole. The snow beneath any tarp can be shoveled out to create a comfortable home for the night. If your tarp requires a pole to hold it up, you'll need something, such as a snow-filled sack or a board, to serve as a platform to keep it from sinking into the snow. The disadvantages of a tarp include its inability to stand freely (as a tent does) and to weather fierce storms. NOLS expeditions in deep snow use snow shelters on most nights, but otherwise use tarps.

When winter camping, make sure that you're packing snow stakes, which are wider and longer than other stakes, to keep them secure in snow. In deep snow, you can use them as deadmen (see page 135).

SLEEPING BAGS

Besides providing comfort, a sleeping bag may be what allows you to survive a frigid night. A bag keeps your body heat near your body by means of the same principles that apply to clothing. Winter sleeping bags are filled with one of two types of insulation: down or a synthetic fiber. Down-filled bags have the best warmth-to-weight ratio, can be stuffed into smaller spaces than synthetics, and cost more than synthetic-filled bags. But remember, if down gets wet, it loses its ability to trap heat, and it is notoriously difficult to dry. If they think they can keep it dry, however, many experienced winter campers choose down. Synthetics are generally easier to maintain in the field, drying more quickly and insulating much better than damp down. And keep in mind that despite your best efforts, long winter expeditions often result in mois-

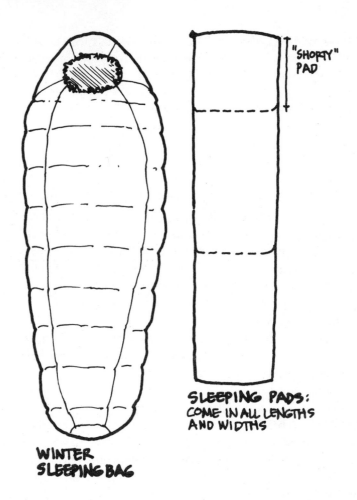

"SHORTY" PAD

SLEEPING PADS: COME IN ALL LENGTHS AND WIDTHS

WINTER SLEEPING BAG

ture slowly collecting in your bag. So if you anticipate a long, icy trip, a synthetic-filled bag is probably the better choice.

Sleeping bags fall loosely into three configurations: mummy, rectangular, and semirectangular. Mummy bags are narrow at the feet, wider at the shoulders, and taper from the shoulders to an insulated hood. They fit snugly around your body like a cocoon, to maximize heat retention; they can be compressed smaller than other shapes but provide less sleeping room. Rectangular bags are squared at the corners, providing plenty of room for tossing and turning, but they let your body heat rush out into the night. They are heavier than mummies, take up more room in your pack, and are seldom chosen by winter campers. Semirectangular bags fall in between, but without an insulated hood, a semirectangular bag is generally no warmer than a rectangular bag. You need a mummy bag in winter. Most bags come in two, sometimes three, lengths. You need to try on a bag to make sure it fits.

Sleeping bags have an outer shell and an inner lining, both of which need to protect you against wind and some water, and they should resist ripping. At the same time, they need to breathe to allow body moisture to escape during the night. Ripstop nylon is relatively windproof, somewhat water-resistant, and strong, and it breathes well. It makes a fine shell. Waterproof, breathable fabrics such as Gore-Tex cost more but make an excellent shell. Nylon taffeta is softer than ripstop and breathes well, but it offers poor resistance to wind and water; it works as a liner.

How the bag is constructed is also important. If the insulation is sewn into quiltlike patches to keep it from shifting around, cold can creep in through the seams. Well-made winter bags are baffled with interior walls that overlap to prevent exposed seams; they should also have draft tubes—long cylindrical compartments filled with insulation—along the zipper and above the chest area.

Another consideration when choosing a sleeping bag is its temperature rating. This tells you how cold it can get outside and still keep you warm inside. As the temperature rating goes down, the price goes up. Unfortunately, the rating is only a guide, and you might feel cold in a bag rated to keep you warm. To be sure, choose a bag rated ten to twenty degrees lower than the coldest temperature you expect to encounter.

SLEEPING PADS

Even if your sleeping bag keeps you warm, you will be miserable sleeping on a poor pad. In fact, you'll probably need two pads, one lying atop the other. The second pad can be a three-quarter length, to protect your head, shoulders, and torso.

Self-inflating pads (such as ThermaRest) offer the most comfort and protection and are your best bet, at least for the top pad. They are available in different widths, lengths, and thicknesses, so be sure to get the right size. Choose one with a nonslip surface to prevent parts of you from slipping off the pad during the night. On the downside, these pads can spring a leak, but the best ones come with repair kits.

NOLS TIP

Use a "Shorty" Pad

A "shorty" is any piece of closed-cell foam big enough to stand on, kneel on (while shoveling snow), sit on, or shove under your hips or shoulders (under your bag) at night. It has other potential uses—some already known, some waiting to be discovered. Having a shorty pad is a great idea.

Closed-cell foam pads are lightweight, relatively comfortable, and virtually indestructible. Like self-inflating pads, they do not absorb moisture, and they cost much less. Two can be used, if you want to avoid the expense and weight of a self-inflating pad; a closed-cell foam pad also makes a great bottom pad beneath an inflating pad. These pads are also excellent as floor mats and bench pads in snow kitchens.

Open-cell foam pads are the least expensive and the least comfortable. They soak up moisture and do not give it back easily. There's no good reason to carry one of these sponges.

SHOVELS AND SAWS

A good snow shovel—one made for mountaineering—is essential for camping in the snow. You'll need one for shelter building, kitchen construction, avalanche safety, and all sorts of odd jobs. The minimal effective size is 9 inches by 12 inches, but moving large quantities of snow becomes tedious with one this small. Shovels closer to a foot square are much more effective snow movers. If you select one with an extendable handle, it will not only pack more easily, but you'll save some stress on your back when you start tossing mounds of the white stuff.

SHOVEL   **SNOW SAWS**

You don't need a snow saw unless you're planning on building one of the snow shelters described in chapter 9. A snow saw is specifically designed for cutting well-sintered snow. It has a relatively small handle (similar to that of a large butcher knife) and a blade about eighteen to twenty-four inches long with large teeth. They can resemble regular hand saws, so be sure to ask for a snow saw when shopping for one for the first time.

FUEL AND STOVE

Before choosing a stove, you need to choose the fuel, and for winter camping, there are only three options: kerosene, butane, and white gas. Kerosene doesn't deserve too much consideration. It's cheap, but it stinks, doesn't produce as much heat as the other two fuels, and tends to coat everything with a greasy film. Butane comes in cartridges that pack

POT

WINDSCREEN

FUEL BOTTLE AND STOVE

neatly, light quickly without priming, and burn cleanly, but butane burns less intensely than white gas, and the cartridges burn inefficiently in the cold. Butane can even freeze in the cartridge on a really cold day. And the cartridges themselves add weight to your pack.

Thus, white gas is almost always the best choice. You always know how much fuel you have (as opposed to a butane cartridge), and after a few trials, you can accurately estimate how much you will need for a trip. Until then, plan on carrying half a quart per person per day, especially if you are melting snow for water. White gas burns very hot and clean and is virtually odorless, no matter how low the temperature falls. Overall, you carry less weight with white gas. It is also available in many countries worldwide, often sold under its chemical name, naphtha.

White gas is not without problems, however. For one thing, it requires priming. Well-made backcountry stoves come with built-in priming mechanisms that almost always work. Squeeze tubes of primer can be purchased for emergencies. If a hot stove blows out in a stiff wind, it is often difficult to restart until it has cooled. White gas stoves require pumping to put the fuel under enough pressure to rise to the burner, and when your hands are cold, you'll hate having to do that.

Another potential problem is the extreme explosiveness of white gas. Extra white gas needs to be stored away from flames, and stoves need to be kept clean and checked often for leaks. If a jet of burning gas erupts from an inappropriate orifice in your stove, run away until it burns itself out.

After you have chosen the fuel, you can select a stove. Once again, there are heaps of choices. Stoves with a plate burner (such as the MSR XGK) usually burn the hottest and the loudest, while stoves with a ported burner (such as the

Optimus 111 Hiker) are a bit slower but quite a bit quieter. Since you may not always want to cook over a blast furnace, a stove that simmers (such as the MSR WhisperLite, which also burns rather quietly, as the name suggests) may be a good choice. If you don't want to spend a lot of time firing up your stove, look for one that lights easily. And since you are concerned about weight, consider the number of ounces that the stove will add to your pack. You will be depending on your stove for a long time, and even the best ones occasionally break down, so choose a stove that you can repair in the field. Carry the appropriate stove repair kit, and practice with it before attempting a repair in the depth of winter.

Accessories are also important. Choose a stove with a windscreen, or buy one separately. And since you'll be cooking on snow, you'll need a stove pad to support the stove evenly and prevent it from disappearing into the melted snow beneath it. You can make a stove pad with a piece of plywood about ten inches square. Cover the top with tin foil,

INSULATED MUG   BOWL

or glue on a piece of Masonite. A piece of closed-cell foam glued to the bottom adds stability. Or you can use the blade of a snow shovel (one that won't melt) as a makeshift pad.

OTHER ESSENTIAL ITEMS

The following ten items are essential on any camping trip in any season:

1. Extra food (more than you think you'll need)
2. Extra clothing (again, more than you expect to need)
3. Map
4. Compass
5. Flashlight and spare batteries (lithium batteries work best in cold)
6. Sun protection (sunglasses, sunscreen, lip protection)

7. First-aid kit
8. Knife or multi-use camping tool
9. Matches or lighter and firestarter (anything flammable that can be used to start a fire; white gas will do)
10. Backup emergency shelter (you're okay with a tent, a tarp, or the skills and tools to build a snow shelter)

In addition, you'll want to carry kitchen gear. Whatever works in other seasons will work in winter. You'll need a large pot if you plan on melting snow for water. If you don't have an insulated mug, get one. Closed-cell foam wrapped around your eating bowl and held in place with duct tape will help retain heat. It's also a good idea to have a wide-mouthed bottle set aside (and well marked) for urination, so you don't have to crawl out of your bag and into the cold.

Because something will probably break or tear, be prepared with repair kits specific to items you're carrying and a general kit with items such as duct tape, bailing wire, a sewing kit, and a few yards of nylon cord.

BASIC WINTER GEAR CHECKLIST

☐ Skis, with skins and a wax kit
☐ Ski poles
☐ Avalanche probe
☐ Pack
☐ Sled and sled harness
☐ Tent or tarp, with snow stakes
☐ Sleeping bag
☐ Sleeping pads (2)
☐ Shovel
☐ Snow saw
☐ Stove, fuel, and platform for stove
☐ The "ten essentials"
☐ Kitchen gear
☐ Repair kits

Chapter 4

A Snow Primer

Familiarity with snow is essential for safe and disciplined winter camping. When the temperature drops below freezing and water vapor condenses into crystals, snow falls. What we call snowflakes are more accurately described as crystals that form around tiny, solid particles in the air, such as dust or salt. As condensed water vapor falls, it encounters a variety of air temperatures, air currents, and humidity levels, and these factors determine what kind of crystals form. Cold, still air usually produces feathery plates or "stellars" the lightest and driest snow, falling with infinite grace and beauty. As the mercury rises, the snow becomes harder, forming needles, columns, dendrites, and, irregular clumps. When the air warms to near freezing, the snow crystals may form into sleet (balls of snow with a hard shell and a soggy center) or hail (solid ice balls that can strike the earth—and winter campers—with ruinous force).

RIME
Technically, rime is not snow at all but rather ice that forms from the freezing of supercooled liquid when it contacts a subfreezing surface. When wind and humidity are particularly high, rime ice may appear as little "flags" that point into the direction of the prevailing wind. At other times, rime ice takes on a wispy look, resembling "snow feathers."

SNOW METAMORPHOSIS

One way to think about snow is to distinguish between snow crystals falling or recently fallen from the sky and those on or in the ground that have been altered by a variety of forces and conditions. In winter, each storm lays down a layer of snow. The accumulated layers, known collectively as the snowpack, meet the atmosphere at a boundary called the snow surface, and they meet the earth at the ground surface.

Snowpacks are prone to constant structural change over time, a process called metamorphosis. Metamorphosis alters the form and structure of snow crystals from the moment they land on earth until they are completely melted. Snow metamorphosis is controlled primarily by temperature, happening quickly near freezing and stopping almost altogether below minus 40 degrees F. Pressure and proximity to the warm ground also participate in metamorphosis, causing snow deep in the snowpack to change faster than snow near the surface. Snow on the surface may change rapidly in response to wind, sun, and other factors. These changes in the snow surface— from powder to ice to slush—make backcountry endeavors both fun and challenging.

Layers within the snowpack may be relatively weak (not well-bonded) or strong (well-bonded). When there is a consistent temperature gradient throughout the snowpack (1 degree C per 10 cm), the crystals, whatever their original forms, consolidate into a well-bonded mass. This is called rounded or equilibrium snow, and the crystals are often just called rounds. A strongly cohesive layer of snow can be cut neatly into blocks for an igloo or shaped creatively into a snow cave or kitchen countertop.

When the temperature gradient within the snow cover is greater, water vapor tends to migrate from the warmer snow close to the ground toward the colder snow at the surface. Under these conditions, entirely new snow crystals, called facets, are formed. Facets tend to crumble in your hand, and are often found by protruding bushes or near the ground in early-season snowpacks. They are common at high altitude, where the snow surface grows colder and a greater gradient is created between surface and ground. Higher elevations also tend to be windier and to avalanche more often, both of which keep the snow thinner and the gradient greater.

Depth hoar (a type of facet) is created early in the season after the first winter storm, usually when temperatures are cold and the sky is clear. It is fragile, collapses easily, and is very noncohesive, constituting a weak layer that is prone to avalanche. You're dealing with depth hoar if you dig into the snowpack and, right before you reach the ground, hit a layer of snow that crumbles at your touch. Depth hoar is most dangerous in the early months of the season; as the snowpack deepens and the pressure on it increases, the danger lessens.

Surface hoar is created on top of the snowpack on nights that are humid, cold, and clear. It is recognizable by its feathery appearance. When buried in a snowpack, it becomes a dangerously thin middle layer that is susceptible to avalanche.

Just as there may be strong or weak bonds within a given layer, entire layers may bond well or poorly to adjoining layers. If two layers are poorly bonded, or if a strongly bonded layer sits atop a weakly bonded one, there is the potential for a slab avalanche (see page 83).

When snow melts and then refreezes, it forms an icy layer that may become a slippery, sliding surface for snow deposited in later storms. This is referred to as melt-freeze metamorphosis. If the melt phase is long enough for water to percolate down through the snow to the ground, a lubricating layer can cover an entire mountainside—a potentially dangerous condition for mountain travelers.

Wind, the greatest mechanical mover of snow, is a powerful change agent. When snow is moved by wind—or by human shoveling or stomping—and is then allowed to set, it hardens through a process called sintering, in which the snow crystals bond firmly together. Old, wind-hammered snow may be thousands of times harder than fresh, powder snow. Sintered snow forms an extraordinarily cohesive layer, one you can walk on without sinking in, and it cuts very nicely into blocks for snow shelters.

Snowpacks developing on slopes undergo another type of mechanical deformation. This deformation occurs because of snow's elasticity (the ability to stretch and return to its original shape) and viscosity (the resistance to free flow) and the force of gravity. Snow tends to flow, or "bend," downhill, a movement called creep. Snow also tends to slide downhill along a slope, a movement called glide. As with metamorphosis, creep and glide are affected by temperature. Snow has minimum viscosity near the freezing point, but as the temperature drops, viscosity increases, and creep and glide slow down. Creep and glide explain some of the marvelous shapes snow can assume.

DRY SNOW VERSUS WET SNOW

The water content of snow is closely related to temperature, and both will impact how easily you can travel through snow-covered terrain. Very dry snow may hold as little as 5% liquid, while wet snow may contain up to 25%. Snow falling at temperatures near the freezing point can weigh three times as much as snow falling at colder temperatures, because it has a much higher water content.

Dry snow (powder) is generally better for traveling, until its depth reaches the point where you are struggling to make headway. After a heavy snowfall of light powder, it may take a day or two for the snow to consolidate enough to keep you on top with skis. It may be spring before it is firm enough to support your weight without skis.

Wet snow not only gets you wet but also adds considerably to your traveling difficulty. Wet snow sticks to skis, crampons, and sometimes boots. Since wet snow falls when the air is relatively warm, it is also difficult to keep from overheating when you are huffing along under a pack. Maritime areas typically receive wet snow, and inland (or "continental") areas receive much drier snow, but early-winter snowfalls in any region can be wet.

One advantage of wet snow is that its frozen surface can often easily be crossed if you travel at night, after the temperature drops, or early in the morning, before the sun softens the surface. When the snow softens, however, you may end up postholing—breaking through the surface up to your knees or higher. If the sunny surface won't support you, try staying in the shade, where the cold lingers longer. If you must posthole, keep your weight on your back leg, step halfway into your next footfall, and wait for the snow to firm up. If postholing overwhelms you, try crawling.

Chapter 5

Traveling in Winter

With skis on feet, pack on back, and sled in tow, you're ready to head out on an adventure in the world of the cold and the white. An untracked vastness awaits, silent but alive, and spec tacular in ways that only the winter traveler will experience. There are challenges ahead, especially if you lack experience in making those boards strapped to your boots move the way you want them to. What follows here is basic information that should be helpful, but as always, you will learn by doing (again, if at all possible, under the guidance of a good teacher).

The most important thing to remember about backcountry skiing is that you can have a great trip even if you are a poor skier. Beyond basic safety, the critical element, at all levels of ability, is fun. The basic idea of backcountry skiing is to move across the snow with as little effort as possible. Forget those pictures of Olympic cross-country skiers gracefully speeding across the finish line, though. You're a winter camper, carrying everything you will need for your adventure, crossing many kinds of "wild" snow, and facing a variety of exciting challenges.

FLAT AND ROLLING TERRAIN
Skiing on flat or relatively gentle, rolling terrain is a skill that comes quickly with just a little practice. As you're moving

along, sliding your feet instead of lifting them, you will soon realize that a push or "kick" off of the back ski sends you gliding forward on the front ski. You've discovered the simplest technique for ski travel: the kick-and-glide.

To improve your kick-and-glide, stay relaxed, and keep your knees slightly flexed and shoulder-width apart. When you "kick" forward, shift all your weight onto the ski you're gliding on and then swing your arm and reach forward with the ski pole on the opposite side from the forward ski. You'll gain a little momentum by pushing with your ski pole, but you should rely primarily on your legs. When the snow is firm, or you're on a track or trail, you can gain speed by double-poling—reaching forward with both poles to get an extra "umph" out of each push. Bend at the waist, and use the mass of your upper body to add momentum. Keep in mind that this technique requires more energy to maintain.

When it's time to change direction on flat terrain, just about anything works if it involves picking up a ski and turning it in the new direction. To do an about-face, use a common method known as the kick turn: (1) Stop, and plant your poles slightly behind you, with the pole on the side you're turning toward between your skis. (2) Lift the ski you'll turn first, kick it out, and swing it entirely around so that it's facing in the opposite direction. (3) Bring the offside pole across and plant it farther away from you than usual. (4) Lift the second ski, bring it around, and shift your ski poles into a more normal position. You end up with both skis pointing in the same new direction.

NOLS TIP

Practice Star Turns

Star turns are an excellent way for your body to learn important muscle movements for skiing. On flat terrain, stick a pole in the snow to serve as a reference point. Face the pole and walk sideways around it, keeping your ski tips pointed toward the pole. Go 360 degrees around the pole, then reverse and walk sideways back around the pole to your starting point. Now face away from the pole and repeat the exercise. Repetition of this fundamental drill will improve your skiing ability.

① PLANT POLES BEHIND YOU

② KICK UP, and TURN ONE SKI INTO THE NEW DIRECTION

SKIS POINT IN OPPOSITE DIRECTIONS

The KICK TURN

③ BRING POLE ACROSS

④ BRING SECOND SKI INTO NEW DIRECTION

⑤ READY TO GO!

The kick turn can be used on just about any terrain (even steep side hills)—as long as you can stop first.

UPHILL TERRAIN

When the terrain gets steeper, you need to shorten your stride and maintain proper balance. The most common mistake made by newcomers is leaning forward on uphill terrain. The center for traction is the center of the ski, under your foot. Leaning forward weights the front of the ski, and you lose traction. Stand up straighter, push down firmly with your heels, keep your stride short (think baby steps), and use your legs as your primary power source (poles are secondary).

UPHILL TECHNIQUES

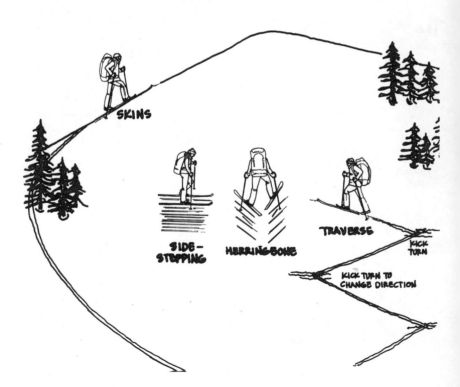

SKINS

SIDE-STEPPING

HERRINGBONE

TRAVERSE

KICK TURN

KICK TURN TO CHANGE DIRECTION

At a certain level of steepness, you need to change your technique, or you'll end up downhill skiing—backward. On firmly packed snow of moderate steepness, you may find the herringbone technique useful. Spread your tips wide, but keep the tails close together, forming a letter V. Roll your knees inward as you climb, digging the inside edges of the skis into the snow. Keep making the letter V again and again as you ascend. Once mastered, the herringbone can get you up short climbs quickly.

Side-stepping is an easier but slower way to ascend short, steep distances, especially when the snow is soft. Stand sideways on the slope, keeping your skis perpendicular to the fall

THE "HERRINGBONE" TECHNIQUE:

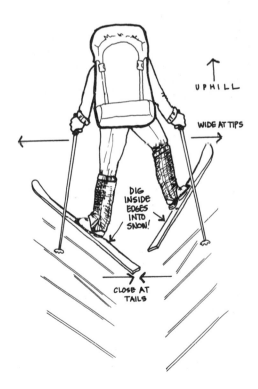

line (the route you would take if you were falling down the slope). Dig your edges into the snow by rolling your knees uphill. Step up with the uphill ski, then bring the downhill ski up beside the uphill ski. For better balance and a little push, hold the downhill ski pole at the top of the grip and shorten your grip on the uphill pole.

Another uphill method, particularly useful on long ascents, involves traversing the hillside—skiing back and forth, gaining a little elevation with each pass, and then doing a kick turn and traversing back, until you reach the top. Performing the kick turns while facing downhill (i.e., turning away from the hillside) is much easier than while facing uphill, and the chance of falling is reduced. With skins, you may be able to negotiate the direction changes of a traverse without a kick turn.

If you anticipate skiing uphill in the backcountry for more than relatively short distances, skins are a necessary piece of gear (see chapter 3). You can climb up amazingly steep slopes with skins (far steeper than wax would allow), and you use a lot less energy. Skins that use glue generally require removal of the kick wax. Otherwise, they may "gum up" and come unglued. Glueless skins can be used directly over your kick wax, but they don't usually glide as well. Because skins in general glide less efficiently than either waxed or waxless skis, most people take them off on flat or downhill terrain.

DOWNHILL TERRAIN

When a downhill run is not too steep, you can just point your skis toward the bottom and go for it. If you feel out of control on the descent, you can always fall—a method of stopping that seldom fails.

With just a bit of practice, you can gain control of a descent on relatively well-packed snow by using the basic snowplow. In the snowplow, you turn your skis into an inverted V, with the point at the tips and the wide part at the tails. By rolling your knees slightly inward, you slide on the inside edges of the skis, while the outsides of the skis "plow" the snow. By shifting your weight to one ski, you slowly turn in the opposite direction. Weighting the right ski, for instance, turns you to the left. Practice the snowplow without a pack before attempting it with a pack.

For many, the best method of controlling a downhill run is by traversing back and forth across the fall line of the slope, losing a little elevation with each traverse. This is the reverse of the uphill method mentioned earlier.

If it's just too steep and icy and otherwise scary, you can take off your skis and hike down the hill. The best way to go down a steep snowfield is to plunge your heels hard into the snow with your knees slightly

FALLING ON SKIS

There are bad ways and good ways to fall. Bad ways include planting your face in the snow and tumbling out of control down a steep incline. The best way to fall is simply to sit down, off to the side, on your buttocks if possible. It hurts less to sit down, and it's easier to get back up from a sitting position. On steep terrain, try to fall to the uphill side. To get up, shift your body around to the front of your skis, slide one foot back, and stand. On an incline, if your skis are uphill, roll over so they're on your downhill side. In deep, soft snow, take your poles off and cross them in the snow, forming the letter X. By holding the poles at the cross of the X, you can support your weight while you regain a standing position. If you're burdened with a heavy pack, you'll probably have to take it off.

bent, a technique known as plunge-stepping. Bend forward at the waist for more stability. Hike off to the side of the slope to prevent gouging holes in the hillside, leaving a clean field for those who might be more daring or accomplished.

For many, the ultimate backcountry, free-heel skiing experience is mastering the telemark turn. Telemark turns are initiated with the body in a low position on the skis. The downhill ski is pushed forward, the leg on that side is flexed so that the knee is over the toes, and the uphill leg is bent so that the heel comes off the ski far enough to point up at the skier's hindquarters. Ideally, the skier's weight remains equally distributed on both legs. When the hips are turned toward the fall line, the skis turn. As the uphill ski becomes the downhill ski, it is turned slightly inward to form a "V" with the other ski, which sharpens the turn. As the turn is completed, reversing the leg positions prepares the skier for the next turn.

When done correctly, the telemark turn is a ferociously lovely maneuver. Learning it involves a lot of practice. You can read about it (see Resources), but to master the telemark turn, you'll need a teacher and lot of time on skis. In the words of author and master tele-skier Allen O'Bannon, "All it takes to be able to ski well in the different conditions possible in the backcountry is time skiing the different conditions in the backcountry."

Wax

As mentioned earlier, no ski is totally waxless: the tip and tail sections of all skis need a glide wax to improve their performance and extend their life. A ski actually melts a microscopic layer of snow underneath it as it slides along. Without glide wax, snow and ice can build up on the bottom of your skis, slowing you down or even stopping you, and unwaxed skis are more easily damaged by snow. Glide wax should be applied with a hot iron at least once a season. It's smart to wax all skis before storing them for the off-season, to prevent drying. Use a wax remover to get rid of the old layer before applying the new wax.

A waxable ski requires a different kind of wax in the kick zone, called kick wax. Kick waxes are softer than glide waxes, giving the ski more grip. For some skiers (racers, for instance), waxing is a complex science involving more than two dozen types of kick waxes. You can get by with just a little knowledge and a simple wax kit: two waxes, a scraper, and a cork.

The correct kick wax for any given snow condition grips the snow when you kick (the ski releases when you glide). In cold temperatures, snow crystals are sharper, and a harder wax is needed for grip. As the temperature rises, crystals grow more rounded, and softer waxes are required. If you used a hard wax in warm temperatures, the ski would slip without gripping. Conversely, using a soft wax in cold temperatures would create too much grip, and snow would stick to the bottom of ski, clumping up to prevent gliding.

Kick waxes are color-coded. The "warm" colors—red and yellow—are softer waxes for warmer snow, when temperatures are above freezing. Purple and blue ("cold" colors) are harder waxes, for temperatures from around the freezing point (purple) down to ten degrees below (blue). Green wax is used when the temperatures are very low. In addition to the basic colors, there are special waxes available for small variances in snow conditions. In most cases, using a two-wax ski system—one for cold, one for warm—is sufficient.

As long as the thermometer registers below freezing, waxing is relatively easy, taking little time. Warmer snow is more difficult to deal with. Klister is a gooey form of wax that works on warm, old snow or ice when nothing else does. Some skiers hate dealing with this messy stuff, but when used well, it can be the ultimate kick wax. Skins are another alternative.

> **N O L S   T I P**
>
> **Use Duct Tape with Klister**
>
> *To reduce the mess of klister:*
>
> 1. *Scrape the kick wax from your ski.*
> 2. *Stick a strip of duct tape on the bottom in the kick zone.*
> 3. *Apply the klister over the tape.*
> 4. *When you no longer need klister, peel off the duct tape, and away it goes.*

The kick zone, where the wax is applied, differs in size, depending on who's applying the wax. Generally, you should wax your skis from a few inches in front of the bindings to the heels of your boots. Some skiers prefer a longer kick zone, especially when hauling a sled, because it "bites" the snow more firmly and allows for a harder kick. In either case, apply the wax with short strokes that run from the tip toward the tail. Multiple thin layers work better than fat gobs. When the kick zone is more or less colored in, you have enough wax on the ski. (New skiers tend to underwax rather than overwax, so be sure to cover the entire kick zone.) Now rub the wax with a

WAXING SKIS

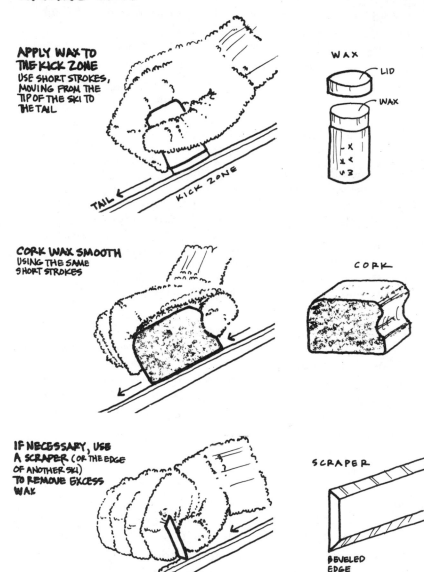

APPLY WAX TO THE KICK ZONE
USE SHORT STROKES, MOVING FROM THE TIP OF THE SKI TO THE TAIL

TAIL

KICK ZONE

WAX

LID

WAX

CORK WAX SMOOTH
USING THE SAME SHORT STROKES

CORK

IF NECESSARY, USE A SCRAPER (OR THE EDGE OF ANOTHER SKI) **TO REMOVE EXCESS WAX**

SCRAPER

BEVELED EDGE

waxing cork, again using strokes from tip to tail. Corking gives you a smoother, more even coat and heats the wax through friction so that it adheres better.

The scraper from your wax kit can be used to scrape off snow adhering to the kick zone. Some scrapers are metal, and some are plastic. Metal ones work faster but increase the chance that you'll remove some of the plastic base of the ski itself. Plastic scrapers take more time but are a safer bet for de-icing. Don't press down too hard when you scrape, or you'll take off all the wax and you'll have to apply a new coating.

BREAKING TRAIL

When there is no trail through the snow, someone has to break one, an ambitious and tiring task, especially in the deep stuff. After each step, you have to free your ski from the snow for the next step. This involves kicking and pulling up until the ski breaks free of the snow, then stepping forward. Leaning back a bit while kicking and pulling usually lends power to the attempt to free the ski.

A group will move faster, and stay happier, if the person breaking trail is relieved periodically. As soon as the trail-breaker tires or feels overheated, she or he steps off the trail and rejoins the group as the last person in line. This type of relay keeps a fresh skier in front, full of energy and psychologically supported by the fact that in fifteen to twenty minutes she or he will be replaced.

When the breaking is really tough—such as in deep snow with a thin crust that supports a skier's weight for a second or two—a group may choose to take turns breaking trail without a pack or sled. One or two skiers move ahead, breaking the trail, then ski back for their packs or sleds, hauling them along a well-groomed track. In some conditions, groups may even choose to break trail one day and move camp down the track the next day.

SKIING WITH A PACK

It's more difficult skiing with a pack than without one, and only practice can refine your skill. The big difference is that your center of gravity shifts farther back. You have to compensate by developing a good packing system. The load should be balanced so that it rides evenly on your center of gravity. The heavier items ride best close to your body, especially when you're skiing. Otherwise, you tend to be pulled backward or thrown sideways. Whether you pack the heavy gear high or low depends on personal preference and terrain. Packing the weight high requires less effort to haul but makes you a little more wobbly—not a problem when the terrain is relatively flat and the skiing is easy. Packing the load low makes your job a bit more strenuous but gives you better balance when the going gets rough or steep.

In a well-organized pack, the load is fitted snugly so that it doesn't shift, throwing you off balance when you least expect it. Everything that you might want on short notice should be readily accessible. You don't want to have to conduct an extended search for your lunch, camera, parka, or asthma medication. Place small items together in a stuff sack to avoid losing them in the depths of your pack. Items such as your sleeping bag can be buried deep. Nothing with hard edges should be placed where it can jab into your back.

SKIING WITH A SLED

A sled helps to manage the weight and bulk of an extended winter expedition. When skiing with one, an important consideration is how you will attach yourself to it. Sometimes, skiers attach their sleds to their packs. This works, but it's better if the sled is attached separately to your hips, in which case you just point the sled in the direction of travel, hook yourself to it, and put on your pack. This way, the pull is more from the core of your body, and therefore easier. This also allows you to throw off the pack, haul the sled up a steep incline, and return for the pack. Finally, a sled attached directly to your hips is easier to turn.

SKIING WITH A SLED

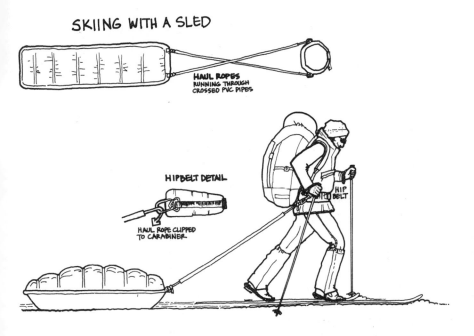

HAUL ROPES
RUNNING THROUGH
CROSSED PVC PIPES

HIPBELT DETAIL

HIP
BELT

HAUL ROPE CLIPPED
TO CARABINER

In open, relatively flat areas, a simple harness system consisting of a couple of towropes tied—or, even better, clipped with carabiners—to the hip belt of your pack will suffice. But the more you need to turn and the steeper the terrain, the more rigid the harness system needs to be to keep the sled from veering back and forth. Rigidity can be supplied by poles, six feet long or so, between you and the sled. You can also create rigid poles for a plastic sled by running two towropes, one from each side of the forward end of the sled, through two lengths of PVC pipe or conduit. (Be careful with PVC in extreme cold, or it will break.) The poles work best in terms of control if they are crossed in the middle, then attached to a well-padded hip belt. The crossover allows you to use natural hip movements to steer the sled into your ski track when you make turns. The crossed poles tend to keep the sled in your track as long as you ski normally.

Loading the sled also requires some ingenuity. First, knock off any ice that might be stuck to the bottom (doing this after loading is unnecessarily difficult). Place a duffel bag in the bottom of the sled, and load the heavy items in the middle with the weight spread out evenly on either side. Pack lighter, bulkier items in the front and back. Your shovel can be lashed to the top of the duffel bag, for quick access. Nylon webbing works great for lashing the bag to the sled, and it should hold the load down tightly so that it won't shift; this also reduces the chance of snagging trees. Keep the lash lines as short and simple as possible, for easy adjustment. Six short straps, for instance, are much easier to handle than one long strap. Rather than threading them around the load and tying knots, use lash straps that are clipped together with quick-release buckles.

On flats and rolling terrain, sled hauling is basically a process of overcoming inertia and keeping it overcome. It usually takes a little jolting pull to start the sled sliding. Once you get going, you can adjust it, if, for instance, you feel it pulling to one side.

Uphills require only a change in effort, primarily in creating long traverses and switchbacks. A well-broken track on the side of a hill may have a small retaining wall that holds the sled in the track. You can also create such a track by slowly and laboriously stomping out a wider-than-usual track. Be sure to have a competent skier up front breaking trail. Despite careful attempts at control, sometimes the sled slips down the slope, so stay attentive and be prepared to stop it. On nasty sidehills, you can put a tether on the back of the sled, so that the person behind you can hold the back up if it starts to slide. If it's a very steep and unavoidable sidehill, try crossing the slope without your sled to "groom" a track for it. When you make a traverse, turning back to cross the same sidehill again, find an area that is free of

---

NOLS TIP

Pace Yourself

When hauling a sled (and even when you're not), use a pace that you can maintain all day. If you can't talk to someone while you're moving, you're breathing too hard and should probably slow down.

trees and not too deep; aim to make more of a U-turn than a kick turn. Seasoned skiers may choose to do an uphill-facing kick turn and then muscle the sled up into a track that now heads off in the opposite direction.

When it comes to downhill runs with a sled, your style is largely determined by your ability to ski. You can race the sled to the bottom and see who wins, or you can let the sled pass you and follow it down. On a wide open slope, some skiers can negotiate slow, gradual turns, keeping the sled somewhat under control. With a long, safe run-out, you may choose to abandon the sled to its own fate and ski down without it. There's one method that never fails: carrying your skis and walking down with your sled.

CROSSING FROZEN WATER

Traveling on the flat, frozen surface of a lake can be a lot easier than struggling through nearby snow, but it is not without hazards, even in northern climes, where the ice may be several feet thick. Springs and swirling currents sometimes create thin ice that is difficult to detect until you plunge through. And snow-covered lakes may be covered with surprisingly thin ice because the snow insulates the surface of the water, preventing it from freezing solid enough to support you. When possible, avoid any lakes that you are unsure of. If you are going to cross a frozen lake, keep these tips in mind:

- Keep your skis on. This disperses your weight over a larger area, reducing the chance that you will break through.
- Spots where streams enter and leave lakes are notorious for thin ice.
- Dark areas are sometimes indicators of thin ice.
- Objects sticking out of the ice, such as logs and rocks, sometimes trap and radiate solar energy, creating weak spots.

SELF RESCUE FROM ICE

EXTEND ARMS PAST THE EDGE OF THE HOLE

PULL YOUR LOWER BODY TO THE SURFACE

KICKING VIGOROUSLY!

(IF YOU HAVE THEM,
USE ICE PICKS TO PULL YOURSELF
ONTO THE ICE)

CONTINUE KICKING AND PULL YOURSELF ONTO THE ICE

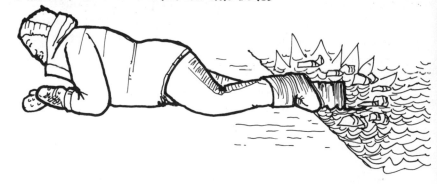

- Tap the ice ahead of you with your ski pole. A solid "thunk" means thick ice, and a hollow "bonk" indicates thin ice.
- Areas shadowed by trees or cliffs usually provide the thickest ice, because the sun has less time to warm them.
- If you fall through, don't panic. Spread your arms wide over the edge of the hole, kick your feet vigorously to get them to the surface, and swim up onto the ice, pulling with your arms as you kick.
- If you anticipate crossing frozen lakes often, carry a pair of ice picks on a string around your neck to facilitate climbing back onto the slippery surface if you fall through.

Fast-moving rivers typically fail to freeze solid enough to support your weight, but slow-moving water may provide excellent pathways in the dead of winter. The tips for crossing frozen lakes apply here as well, plus the following:

- Avoid ice over the fastest current, which is easier said than done. The strongest current—and the weakest ice—tends to lie on the outside of bends and where the river drops.
- Wind-scoured ice tends to be weaker than ice in sheltered areas.
- If you think the water is deep enough to submerse you, don't cross. A breakthrough may cause you to be sucked under the ice.
- Look for braids in the river where the flow separates into two or more narrow channels. These generally offer a few narrow, shallow crossings.

Additionally, if you're able to determine the depth of the ice, keep in mind the following minimum safe depths:

MINIMUM DEPTHS FOR CROSSING ICE SAFELY

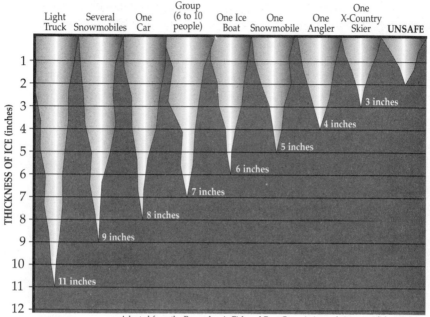

Adapted from the Pennsylvania Fish and Boat Commission website, www.fish.state.pa.us

GETTING FOUND

Despite your best efforts, you may end up someplace you don't want to be: lost. If that happens, keep a positive mental attitude—panic can kill. Stop, relax, and devise a plan. A calm mind thinks more rationally and creatively. Actively participate in staying warm, fed, and hydrated and in getting found. Keep your group together, and make reasonable efforts to get oriented.

One useful technique is to backtrack to a point where your location was definitely known. This is a relatively simple process in snow if you follow your ski trail. If backtracking fails, send out scouting parties of two or more in an attempt to determine your location. Each party needs to have an exact scouting plan and should return to the starting point in about thirty minutes. At least one person should remain at the starting point. If your location can be determined with certainty, and if weather and group strength are acceptable, move toward the intended destination. Avoid shortcuts or any line of travel that would hide the group from a search party. If your location cannot be determined, stay put.

It is important to stay as visible as possible. Stop moving before dark and choose a campsite that is protected from the weather but still visible to searchers. Camp in the open, near packed ski trails. If possible, build large, smoky fires that can be seen from the air or the ground. Listen for the sounds of searchers or other winter travelers. Make noise by singing, whistling, or shouting to attract attention.

If a plane is searching overhead, a bright flash of light is most easily seen from the air. Mirrors are therefore effective signaling devices, and some compasses come with signal mirrors. Bright flashes can also be created by reflecting the sun off pot or pan lids, jewelry, or other metal objects. Remember that moving people are easier to spot than immobile people, and people out in the open are easier to spot than people standing under trees. From the air, brightly colored items—sleeping bags, rain gear, parkas—laid out in the open are more visible than people waving their arms. Geometric patterns are even more visible than bright colors are.

Chapter 6

Winter Hazards

Winter travelers need to be lifelong students of winter hazards. In addition to the possibility of harm, or even death, related to the cold of winter (see chapter 8), there are numerous hazards associated with winter storms and the accumulation of tremendous amounts of snow. The wise winter camper is ready to deal with—or, even better, avoid—dangerous winter weather and avalanches.

WINTER WEATHER

One way to minimize the hazards of winter weather is to anticipate what's coming. Experienced winter travelers are usually amateur meteorologists. Before you travel into an area, familiarize yourself with the prevailing weather conditions, including the most severe conditions ever encountered in that region. Regions tend to exhibit weather patterns that vary seasonally but are reasonably consistent from one year to the next. Winds, for instance, may blow prevailingly from one direction, influencing your choice of campsites and routes. The bottom line: knowing regional climate and weather patterns can be just as useful, or even more so, as knowing a specific day's forecast.

But of greater significance is what is actually going on in the sky above you and the air around you. The clouds, pressure changes, temperature changes, and air movement are constantly sending messages to you.

Clouds

The sky can reveal vital information in the form of clouds. Clouds generally come in three basic forms: cirrus, cumulus, and stratus.

High, wispy cirrus clouds—sometimes known as mare's tails—are made of ice crystals and are often on the leading edge of a warm front, usually bringing in some type of change in the weather.

Puffy, white cumulus clouds are typically fair-weather clouds. They may bring nothing more than some wind and an opportunity to see pictures in the sky. But if they thicken, tower upward, and darken into cumulonimbus clouds, a storm is building. If they tower up to the cirrus layer, winds will shear off their tops, giving them a dark, anvil shape.

Stratus clouds appear as one or more horizontal layers of clouds. They tend to be low and fast moving, and they may be accompanied by strong wind. They often signal a change in the weather: a storm could be building, or a storm could be leaving.

A lenticular cloud—a "cap" of cloud that forms like a giant upside-down bowl above a peak—tells you that a mountain's upper elevations are getting hammered by very strong, cold winds. It also warns that precipitation is likely to follow within forty-eight hours.

Also, take notice if there's a wide halo surrounding the moon by night or the sun by day. It indicates that precipitation may begin within a day or two. If the ring is narrow and tight, the precipitation might be no more than twelve hours away.

The Air

There are two types of air masses—warm and cold—that influence all weather. When a warm front (a mass of warm air)

CLOUD TYPES

CIRRUS

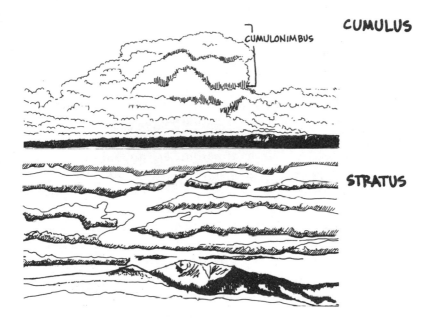

CUMULUS

CUMULONIMBUS

STRATUS

LENTICULAR

moves in, the warm air drifts in above the colder air that is already there, forming thin clouds. If the warm air rises fast enough, the clouds may thicken and drop snow. If a cold front (a mass of cold air) bullies its way in below warmer air, it causes the warm air to rise quickly, which tends to form clouds heavy with moisture, and precipitation falls. Thus, cold fronts are more often associated with rapid weather changes and more dramatic storms.

Air pressure is the weight of the atmosphere pressing down on the surface of the planet. It is measured by a barometer in inches of mercury or in units called millibars. A high-pressure system means heavier air, and that usually brings cooler temperatures and clear skies. A low-pressure system brings the opposite: a warm air mass, with warmer temperatures and resulting storms. In nice weather, the barometric pressure rarely drops much below 30 inches of mercury. If the barometric pressure starts to fall, it means that clouds are going to build and precipitation is going to fall. A rise in barometric pressure usually indicates the opposite: clearing skies. If you don't have a barometer, an altimeter can sometimes substitute—if you remember to think in reverse. Although altimeters can be affected by other factors, such as heat, if an altimeter shows an increase in altitude (when you are not rising), it generally means that the barometric pressure is falling, and a storm front may lie just over the horizon. An altimeter that falls when you've stayed level indicates rising pressure.

In addition to air pressure, the temperature of the air is relevant. Many of the challenges of winter camping arise from the air temperature and the fact that it goes hand in hand with wind and other changes in the immediate environment. Temperature can alter the surface of the snow—for example, from firm to slushy—and thus change the speed at which you travel. Temperature also affects what you wear, where you camp, how much you eat, and how you feel.

On a typical day, in the absence of big weather changes, the air warms slowly throughout the hours of sunshine.

Shortly after sundown, the temperature starts to drop, reaching its low point just before sunrise. As you gain altitude, both the temperature and the barometric pressure drop, a normal phenomenon.

Wind

Wind is a tremendous challenge to winter travelers. Although it can sculpt snow into wondrous shapes, you'll often prefer that it do so when you're somewhere else. Wind can blind you, tear away precious body heat, and suck up your energy like a gigantic vacuum cleaner.

Winds can be prevailing, or they can be determined by topography. Prevailing winds are air movements that are consistent in a given area in a given season. In the latitudes of the United States, the prevailing movement of air is west to east. Some winds can be remarkably predictable in direction, strength, and timing. Topography can change the character of wind. When wind slams up against a mountain or a ridge, for instance, the moving air is forced to flow up and over the land. This "orographic lifting" channels the wind through the first break in the land, such as a mountain pass, or up and over a ridge. This phenomenon explains why the wind through mountain passes, on summits, and along the crest of a ridge may blow with considerably more ferocity than the wind even a short distance below the summit or off the ridge. A topographical map allows you to guess where you are likely to encounter the worst winds—passes, summits, ridge crests, and slopes on the windward side of mountains, and high plateaus on the leeward side of passes.

When the wind blows, the air feels colder. And the harder the wind blows, the colder you feel. The temperature of the air stays the same, whether it is moving or not, but you feel colder because moving air dissipates heat faster than still air does. The wind chill index, most recently revised in 2000, is an indicator of how fast exposed skin cools off at a given air temperature when the wind is blowing at a given speed. For example, at an air temperature of 5 degrees F and a wind

WIND CHILL INDEX

	TEMPERATURE (°F)																	
Calm	40	35	30	25	20	15	10	5	0	-5	-10	-15	-20	-25	-30	-35	-40	-45
5	36	31	25	19	13	7	1	-5	-11	-16	-22	-28	-34	-40	-46	-52	-57	-63
10	34	27	21	15	9	3	-4	-10	-16	-22	-28	-35	-41	-47	-53	-59	-66	-72
15	32	25	19	13	6	0	-7	-13	-19	-26	-32	-39	-45	-51	-58	-64	-71	-77
20	30	24	17	11	4	-2	-9	-15	-22	-29	-35	-42	-48	-55	-61	-68	-74	-81
25	29	23	16	9	3	-4	-11	-17	-24	-31	-37	-44	-51	-58	-64	-71	-78	-84
30	28	22	15	8	1	-5	-12	-19	-26	-33	-39	-46	-53	-60	-67	-73	-80	-87
35	28	21	14	7	0	-7	-14	-21	-27	-34	-41	-48	-55	-62	-69	-76	-82	-89
40	27	20	13	6	-1	-8	-15	-22	-29	-36	-43	-50	-57	-64	-71	-78	-84	-91
45	26	19	12	5	-2	-9	-16	-23	-30	-37	-44	-51	-58	-65	-72	-79	-86	-93
50	26	19	12	4	-3	-10	-17	-24	-31	-38	-45	-52	-60	-67	-74	-81	-88	-95
55	25	18	11	4	-3	-11	-18	-25	-32	-39	-46	-54	-61	-68	-75	-82	-89	-97
60	25	17	10	3	-4	-11	-19	-26	-33	-40	-48	-55	-62	-69	-76	-84	-91	-98

WIND (mph) — vertical axis label

FROSTBITE TIMES   □ 30 minutes   ■ 10 minutes   ■ 5 minutes

speed of 25 miles per hour, your skin cools at a rate equivalent to a still air temperature of minus 17 degrees F. The index also calculates how fast frostbite can occur to exposed skin at different wind chill temperatures.

Whiteouts

Mountain clouds sometimes appear out of thin air, and mountain snow can fall with impenetrable thickness. Either way, the air turns the same milky white as the featureless, snow-covered ground, reducing visibility to zero. When you lose the ability to tell earth from sky, you are in a whiteout. Whiteouts occur where the terrain lacks trees or other vegetation. They are always terribly disorienting, and they can be dangerous. You cannot see a sudden drop-off in front of you, find the way to your intended destination, or even be sure which way is up.

If the sky seems to be building toward a whiteout, and you have noted major landmarks—ridges, cliffs, trees, ravines—you can take a compass bearing and head for a destination through the whiteout. Nonetheless, if you have a choice, it's always best to hunker down and wait it out when confronted with a whiteout.

AVALANCHES

An avalanche is any significant mass of snow in motion down the side of a mountain. Avalanches vary from small sluffs that run no more than fifty yards to gigantic climax avalanches. Most avalanche victims are unable to identify high-risk terrain or unstable snow conditions, and even some experienced people get complacent and stop paying attention. When there is a slope, a sufficient load of snow, a weak layer, and a triggering nudge, an avalanche occurs. There are excellent books available on avalanches (see Resources), but some basic, important information is presented here.

Whatever their size, avalanches fall into one of two general types, determined by the character of the snow at the origin of the slide. The first type, a loose snow or point release avalanche, originates at a single point, or in a small area, and fans out as it moves downhill. Within a loose snow avalanche, there is poor cohesion among the snow crystals. Sometimes it is so loose that you cannot detect a line separating the snow that avalanched from the snow that stayed put. Loose snow slides when the angle of the slope is too steep for the snow crystals to stick. These avalanches typically have little destructive power—except in the warmer months, when they may be quite wet—but they can carry a skier over a cliff or into sharp rocks.

The second type, a slab avalanche, starts when a large mass of highly cohesive snow breaks away. There is an obvious fracture line, called the crown, where the slab separates from the snow above it. Fracture lines also mark the flanks—the sides of the avalanche's path. At the lower end of the slab, where it breaks away from and overrides the stable snow, there may be a line of failure, called the stauchwall. The slab may slide along the ground, but it usually fails to bond to a less cohesive layer of snow beneath it. This less cohesive layer, called the weak layer, lies above the bed, or sliding, surface on which the avalanche rides. Slab avalanches can be soft or hard. Soft slabs break apart after starting to slide, taking on the appearance of a large, loose snow avalanche. Hard slabs

LOOSE SNOW AVALANCHE

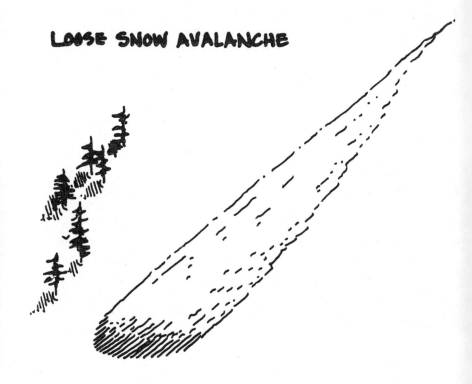

tend to break into blocks of snow that retain some of their angularity. Slab avalanches are the greatest source of life-threatening danger in snowy mountains.

Terrain determines the path the avalanche will follow, but the paths of all slab avalanches (and some loose snow avalanches) can be divided into three zones. The starting zone is where the avalanche starts and picks up speed. Along the track, the middle zone of the path, the snow slides at a relatively constant speed, unless altered by bold terrain changes, and little or no snow is deposited. Below the track lies the deposition zone, where the snow decelerates and finally stops.

Objectively, avalanches are just another way in which all things seek a natural balance. Although it is impossible to

SLAB AVALANCHE

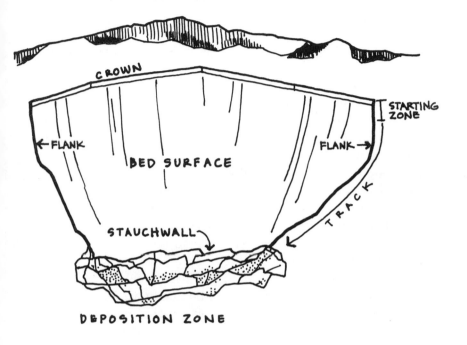

know exactly when an avalanche will occur, you can make a well-educated guess. To be safe, you need to learn to recognize and avoid avalanche danger.

Assessing Avalanche Risk

Before heading into avalanche terrain, investigate the risk for the specific time of year. As a public service, some mountain regions provide general information about avalanche danger. More specific details should be obtained from the nearest governmental land management agency. Daily avalanche reports that assess risk are available on the Internet for many regions, but keep in mind that your terrain might differ from that covered in the report. Additional information is often available from local ski areas, outdoor shops, newspapers, and radio stations.

Avalanche hazards are rated as follows:

Low. Generally stable snow, with isolated areas of instability.

Moderate. Areas of unstable snow, possible on steep terrain, with human-triggered avalanches possible.

Considerable. Unstable slabs probable on steep terrain or on certain aspects, with human-triggered avalanches probable and natural avalanches possible.

High. Unstable snow likely on a variety of aspects and slope angles, with natural and human-triggered avalanches likely. Travel is not recommended.

Extreme. Extremely unstable slabs widespread on most slopes and slope angles, with avalanches certain on some slopes. Travel should be avoided.

Remember, whatever the generally perceived risk of an avalanche, specific slopes may be ready to slide at any moment, and a rating of "low" does not eliminate the chance of an avalanche. At the same time, "extreme" does not rule out the possibility of having a lovely time in gentle terrain.

Identifying Avalanche Zones

To avoid avalanche terrain, you need to know what it looks like. Most importantly, avalanche terrain lies on a slope. The question is, how steep must a slope be to avalanche? Wet, sloppy avalanches have occurred on slopes as shallow as ten degrees. Even this type of slide can be dangerous if it pushes you over a cliff or buries you. Wind-hardened slabs have fallen off mountainsides as steep as sixty degrees, but snow on such steep terrain usually sloughs off before it consolidates into avalanche proportions. Studies indicate that the majority of avalanches occur on slopes that fall in the range of thirty to forty-five degrees.

Relatively accurate measurements of a slope's angle can be taken with an inclinometer, an easy-to-use, inexpensive

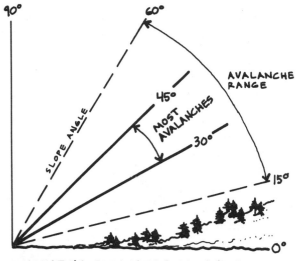

EVALUATING RISK WITH SLOPE ANGLES

plastic device that usually comes with directions printed on the face. Relatively inaccurate guesses can be made by holding your index finger and thumb at a right angle and lining up the slope where the finger and thumb meet. If the slope approximately divides the ninety-degree angle of finger and thumb, the slope is roughly forty-five degrees. Steeper slopes lie closer to your index finger, and gentler slopes lie closer to your thumb. Fortunately, almost everyone overestimates slope angle using this method.

Another important factor in the identification of dangerous terrain is the profile of the slope—straight, convex, or concave. Any straight slope, open and covered in snow, can be an avalanche waiting to happen, and the slide can start anywhere. If the slope is convex, flexed up toward the sky, the chance of an avalanche is even greater. That convex bulge enhances tensile stress, a stretching tension created within the mass of snow by its tendency to creep downhill. If a crack occurs at the point of highest stress, usually just below the bulge, the snowpack can slide downhill. A concave slope is

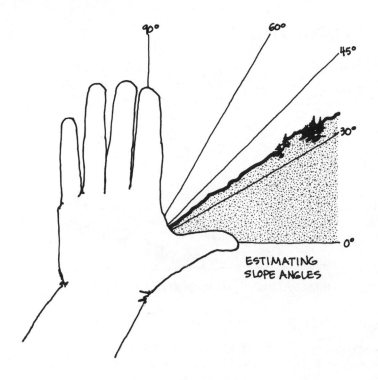

ESTIMATING
SLOPE ANGLES

generally considered safer than a convex slope, because hard snow at the bottom of the slope supports the snow higher up. However, soft snow or snow resting on depth hoar at the bottom of a concave slope may give way with the weight of a traveler, upsetting the snow balance on the slope above and causing it to slide.

Couloirs (narrow gullies filled with snow), drainages (depressions low enough that water drains into them), and other slope irregularities form natural avalanche pathways. A topographic map can be an essential tool in identifying and avoiding such terrain traps. Climbers are especially susceptible to couloir avalanches, because these gullies also form natural pathways up a mountain. The release zone above the gully, where storms may have deposited a huge mass of snow, may be difficult to evaluate from below. A gully, even a shallow one, on an open slope is a perfect place for snow to

CONVEX SLOPE

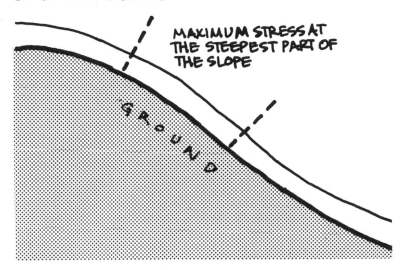

MAXIMUM STRESS AT
THE STEEPEST PART OF
THE SLOPE

GROUND

CONCAVE SLOPE:

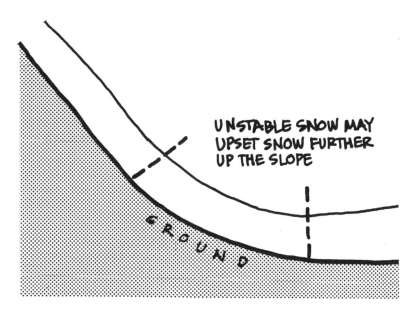

UNSTABLE SNOW MAY
UPSET SNOW FURTHER
UP THE SLOPE

GROUND

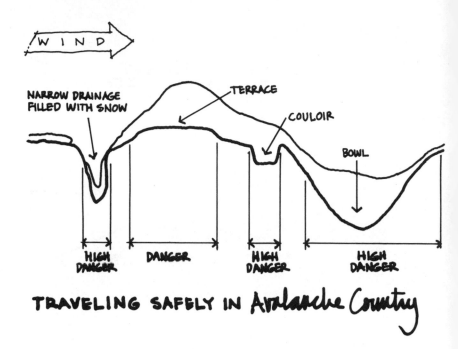

TRAVELING SAFELY IN Avalanche Country

deposit and consolidate into a tense, avalanche-prone slab.
Snow-filled bowls also create traps for the unwary. Their
beautifully sloping sides are a siren's call to skiers, but those
same sides trap heavy snow deposits, which harden and avalanche easily. Bowls often have narrow outlets where the sliding snow builds up in natural terrain traps.

Terraces, or benches, may form natural barriers to an avalanche. Early in the snow season, a terrace is a tempting path
for mountain travelers, but the same terrace may create a deposition zone for a slide from above and a burial ground for the
unwary. An outcropping of rock, forming an island of refuge,
is sometimes a safe stopping place in an avalanche zone. It is
far better, however, to avoid an avalanche zone altogether.
Wide valleys may offer safe routes of travel. Narrow
drainages can act as traps as avalanching snow piles up in the
bottom. The questions to answer are: How much snow is
above you? How stable is the snow? How wide is the run-out

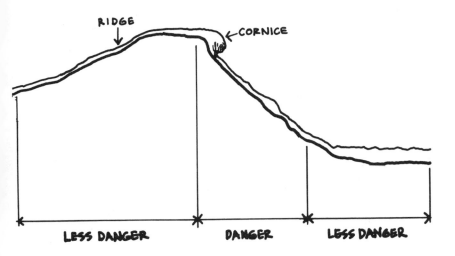

zone? Stay well away from narrow drainages with sloping, snow-covered sides.

Ridges offer the safest routes. On narrow ridges, be aware of cornice formation. Cornices are overhanging lips of snow created by wind, and are often hidden from travelers on the ridge. The lip of snow "grows" from the ridgetop out, in the opposite direction of the prevailing wind, so the cornice overhangs the leeward side of the ridge (the side sheltered from the wind). Thus, it is safer to travel on ridges on the windward side (the side facing into the wind). Avoid traveling under cornices as well—they sometimes break off naturally, triggering an avalanche.

Underneath the snow, the surface of the slope is another factor determining whether the snow will slide, especially early in the season. As a general rule, the rougher the slope surface, the more snow it takes to create an avalanche. Thus, grassy slopes and smooth rock surfaces avalanche more easily. These surfaces, if they are steep enough, often avalanche to the ground several times during the snow season. Bushes and small trees, such as willows, usually anchor the snowpack early in the season, until they are buried. Later, under heavy snow, light vegetation is crushed by the weight and bent downhill by the creep of the snow cover, adding little to snow stabilization. Dense vegetation may actually trap air near the ground, encouraging the formation of depth hoar and providing a weak layer above the ground surface. Trees, if they are thin enough to ski through easily, will not deter an avalanche. Slopes covered with thick timber are usually safe but may be virtually impossible to ski through. Remember to look above the timber as well, taking note of the possibility of a huge slab breaking off an open slope with enough mass to destroy the tree cover or push through it.

The orientation of a mountain's face to the sun and wind helps determine whether the snow cover will slide. In the Northern Hemisphere, south-facing slopes get the full force of the sun, while north-facing slopes lie in shadow most of the day. Because south slopes get more sunlight, snow metamorphosis (see chapter 4) progresses at a faster rate there than on north slopes. Snowpacks consolidate more quickly after a storm, making them either avalanche or stabilize sooner, both of which make south slopes a generally safer bet for travel from the beginning to the middle of the season. But later in the season, as temperatures rise and snow begins to melt, south slopes are prone to wet avalanches, and the risk of traveling them increases. North slopes, with little exposure to sunlight, remain cooler, resulting in a retardation in metamorphosis. Cooler temperatures also increase the chance of depth hoar and facet formation and the persistence of these weak layers. Therefore, north slopes remain dangerous longer after a storm, but for a brief period toward the end of the season, when wet snow is sliding off south faces. Latitude has an effect on both slopes. For example, south faces in the southern Rocky Mountains get more solar radiation than do slopes with the identical orientation in the northern Rockies. Greater radiation creates a higher rate of recrystallization of snow, which tends to produce thin, weak layers that form sliding surfaces for avalanches. These factors in turn influence regional avalanche patterns.

Wind plays an extraordinarily important role in the formation of avalanches. Wind moves snow around, and, once disturbed, the snow sinters into slab consistency. Mountain travelers need to be aware of the wind's prevailing direction to avoid avalanche-prone slopes. When wind can be felt or blowing snow can be seen, determining wind direction is easy. In the absence of wind, mountains offer subtle reminders of where the wind once blew. Cornices, like windsocks at an airport, point out the wind's direction. Sometimes, however, swirling winds create double-corniced ridges, with windsocks in both directions. Around trees, rocks, and other things that stick out of the snow, the wind builds drifts. Snow piles up on the windward side of such objects, and long tails stretch out on the leeward side, indicating the wind's direction. On open surfaces, hard winds may carve sastrugi—intricate, fantastic shapes formed in snow. The steeper, sharp faces of sastrugi point into the wind, and the broader tails fan out on the leeward side. Also keep an eye out for rime (see page 51), which always builds up on the windward side of objects, pointing into the prevailing wind. The greater the amount of rime and the taller it is, the higher the wind.

Windward slopes have less snow deposited on them than leeward slopes do. Because the snow is wind-scoured, it is usually safer. In windy conditions, leeward slopes gather snow quickly, whether there is fresh snow falling or not. Rapid snow deposition makes leeward slopes far more unstable and dangerous and more prone to natural avalanches than windward slopes are.

Finally, terrain that has had one avalanche is likely to have another. Keep an eye out for steep, open mountainsides, bare swaths of snow cutting through a stand of timber, stands of saplings running through an older forest, and steep gullies with no growth in them. Look out for trees that are torn and scarred, with limbs ripped off on the uphill side, and tops missing. Watch for piles of dirty snow, with debris and uprooted trees mixed in, at the bottom of slopes. Check slopes ahead for fracture lines where an avalanche started but lacked the impetus to continue.

Avoiding Avalanches

Safety in avalanche terrain is both an art and a science. The most dangerous route of travel is one where you may be the trigger for an avalanche. Stay away from avalanche release zones, avalanche paths, leeward slopes, cornices, narrow drainages, and other terrain traps. Stay off of steep slopes, especially inclinations of thirty degrees or more, and particularly if the slope profile is convex. Avoid steep slopes with thin stands of timber that you can easily pass through. And remember, during and immediately after a big storm, all mountainous areas should be considered unsafe, and the lower the temperature, the longer the hazard will persist. Do not camp or even take rest breaks in an area of avalanche danger.

As noted earlier, the safest route of travel is on top of a ridge and toward the windward side, above avalanche release zones. The second safest route is down the middle of a wide valley, away from deposition zones. Thick stands of timber may offer a safe but bothersome route.

If your intended route will cross a slope that might avalanche, reconsider: Is there an alternative route? If the slope does avalanche, what will the outcome be? Is it worth the risk?

If you must cross an avalanche slope, choose the safest route and avoid the most likely trigger zones. Snow tends to break off at points of greatest stress: near the top of a straight slope, at the steepest point of a convex slope, where an irregularity in the terrain (rocks, trees) breaks the snow surface. If you must ascend or descend to reach the starting point of the safest route, go up or down on safe snow near the slope. If the dangerous slope itself must be ascended or descended to reach the starting point, follow the fall line instead of cutting across it. This means going straight up or straight down, off to one side of the slope. If skis make this difficult, take them off and plow through the snow. If there are islands of safety on the slope, such as rock outcroppings or dense stands of timber, plan a route from one safe area to the next. On an open slope, stay high, where there is less snow to slide down from above.

Traverse the slope diagonally—not horizontally—from the top toward the bottom. Horizontal cuts are more likely to tempt the snow to slide. And try to avoid turns that take you back under an already potentially weakened slope. Ski turns add stress to the slope.

Everything that an avalanche could catch and hold should be easy to shed. Loosen pack straps and undo hip belts, loosen bindings on snowshoes and skis, and remove wrist loops on ski poles. Tighten clothing, put on a hat, pull up the parka's hood, and slip on mittens. If you are caught in an avalanche and snow gets inside your clothing, your body will cool faster, shortening survival time.

If you have electronic rescue transceivers, make sure that they are working, are turned to transmit, and are secured somewhere on each person, not in a pack that could be torn off. This should be done before you begin skiing for the day.

When everyone is ready, cross one at a time, with at least one person serving as a spotter at all times. The spotter and victim can yell if an avalanche breaks loose, and the spotter can watch the victim until he or she comes to rest or goes under. Generally, it is best for everyone to take the same trail across, but with a large party, avoid following the trail too precisely, which may cut a deep trench through the snow and break loose a slab. Don't stop until you have reached a safe spot.

Surviving an Avalanche

It is strongly recommended that at least one member—if not all members of your group have passed a Level I recreational avalanche course; training is typically given in a four-day seminar involving classroom work and field practice. However, staying alive in avalanche country requires you to become an ongoing student of avalanche safety and survival.

If the worst happens, and the snow starts to slide, the most direct route toward safety should be taken. There may be time for you to ski or run to the side of the avalanche path, where the snow is probably shallower and moving a little slower. Once the snow underfoot starts to break up, you will quickly sink into the churning mass, losing all hope of moving out of the way. This is a good time to scream as loudly as possible to alert companions to your distress. If there are trees or rocks that can be grabbed and held on to, try to do so.

Once you are caught in the moving snow, all equipment that can be thrown off probably should be, although some experts say that small day packs may be advantageous, protecting your back and providing some flotation. Packs, skis, ski poles, and snowshoes often become anchors dragging you under the frozen flood. As you are swept along, try to swim. There is no officially approved avalanche-swimming stroke; try anything—back stroke, dog paddle, treading wildly—to keep your head "above water." If you feel your feet hit a hard surface, push off aggressively in an attempt to regain the surface. If your head goes under, keep your mouth shut and try not to breathe. A mouth or nose full of snow could solidify enough to form a firm plug. Should there be a moment when your head is in the open air, however, take in a deep breath.

As the slide starts to slow down, make a desperate effort to reach the surface. If that doesn't work, vigorously try to create a breathing space by shaking your head, getting a hand up to your face to push the snow away, and wiggling around to make room for your chest to move (but keep your mouth shut). While movement is still possible, try to thrust one hand toward the surface. Remember, most victims are found because something sticks out above the snow.

Now comes the hard part—waiting. Survival is more likely if you stay calm: panic increases the body's need for oxygen. The snow will quickly sinter into the consistency of stone, making efforts to get free a waste of priceless oxygen and valuable energy. Even partially buried victims are often unable to dig themselves out without help. If you feel unconsciousness descending, don't try to fight it. Unconsciousness reduces the body's need for oxygen and energy requirements.

If you witness someone caught in an avalanche, attach your eyes to the place where the victim was last seen until that spot can be safely marked with something, such as a ski or a ski pole. If there is the danger of further avalanching, someone should be posted as a lookout to yell a warning to rescuers as the search gets under way. This is a situation in which good leadership is vital. The leader needs to be sure not only that everything possible is being done for the victim but also that everything possible is being done to keep the others safe.

If the victim was carrying a transceiver, before any attempt at probing, turn the other units to receive, and begin an appropriate transceiver rescue. Not all rescue transceivers work exactly the same way, and competence in using them should be attained before going into the field. The transceiver search has two phases: a hasty search for the signal, and a detailed search for the burial point. You should be able to

SEARCHING FOR AN AVALANCHE VICTIM

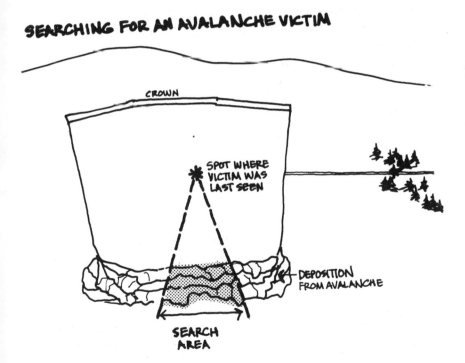

CROWN

SPOT WHERE
VICTIM WAS
LAST SEEN

DEPOSITION
FROM AVALANCHE

SEARCH
AREA

perform both of these searches in less than three minutes (less than two minutes if you excel).

Without transceivers, a hasty search of the area should begin as soon as the snow has stabilized. Search at the last-seen spot and on the slope below that spot. Mark places where pieces of the victim's equipment are found. The surface provides the most important clues leading to the buried victim. Which way was the victim probably carried by the avalanche? Where might the victim have gotten stuck on the way down? Victims often lodge on the uphill sides of trees and rocks or spiral out below them. Use avalanche probes, ski poles, or skis to probe in the most likely spots.

If the hasty probe search turns up nothing, begin a more systematic probing search (called a coarse probe). Just two or three rescuers can quickly and efficiently probe the highest-priority areas—where the slide debris is heaviest, benches where the slope flattens before continuing down, and the slope below markers denoting pieces of the victim's equipment. Probe searches usually work best if they go up the slope, along the most likely descent line of the victim. Searchers should stand elbow to elbow, and probe, step, probe, step. If there are fewer searchers, they can stand an arm's length apart and probe right, probe left, step, repeat. When the probe hits a rock or a frozen tree, the rescuer will be able to feel the hardness of the object. When the probe hits a person, there is a softer, more giving feel. If the probe hits a buried victim, leave it in place and dig as rapidly as possible.

OTHER WINTER HAZARDS
Hidden Rocks and Logs
Snow hides things, and obstacles buried beneath the snow can become hazards if you collide with them. For example, you could ski into a submerged log at ankle height—and snap goes your ankle.

You can significantly reduce, but not completely eliminate, the risk of injury by skiing a packed track. Skiers who stay on trails seldom encounter obstacles beneath the snow. Off-trail or off-track, watch for subtle high or low spots in the snow. High spots may be snow mounded over rocks or logs. Low spots, or depressions in the snow, may indicate a hole between rocks or logs that could catch and hold your skis.

Tree Wells

As the sun warms tall trees that stick out above the snow, a bowl-like depression is created around the tree by melting snow. These tree wells aren't found in dense, shadowed forests but rather where trees grow farther apart and the sun can reach down to snow level. When the snow is deep, and as the days grow longer and warmer (late winter, early spring), tree wells can reach substantial depths. To make things worse, periods of melting and freezing may turn the walls of the wells into sheets of ice. So if you ski into one, you may be unable to stop and find yourself hitting the tree with great force. Avoiding tree wells is simple: pay attention. They're easy to see, if you keep your eyes peeled, and they're easy to ski around.

Undercut Snow

Another dangerous manifestation of the white stuff is called undercut snow. Snow underneath the surface sometimes melts before the surface does—usually in late winter or early spring—due to solar heat radiating from submerged rocks or other objects or water, such as a creek, running beneath the snow. What is left is a bridge of snow over a hole, which you discover when, without warning, the snow collapses and you drop into it. The danger comes primarily from what lies at the bottom of undercut snow—rocks, logs, rough ground, or water.

Any time the temperature is above freezing and there are creeks or boulder fields, you need to watch out for undercut snow. Stay well away from running water and from rocks or other objects sticking out of the snow. Watch for signs that someone or something has punched through a snow bridge. If you can't avoid an area that may hide undercut snow, move slowly and probe ahead with ski poles. The fact that you're traveling on skis will help, as they disperse your weight and lower the risk that you'll break through.

Chapter 7

Water and Food in Winter

An adequate intake of water and food—critical not only to life on the trail but also to life everywhere else—assumes even more importance as the temperature falls. The colder the environment, the greater your need for energy—energy to carry on the processes of life, to move through the frigid landscape, and to stay warm enough to avoid the hazards of excessive cold (see chapter 8).

HYDRATION

Your body is about two-thirds water. The blood coursing through your body is about 90% water; it not only carries oxygen and nutrients to cells (and waste products away) but also transfers warmth from heat-generating areas, such as hardworking muscles, to areas that need it, such as your head, fingers, and toes. Water is necessary for breathing, as it moisturizes the dry air you suck into your lungs. It is also needed for cell metabolism—the source of energy and, therefore, heat—and to keep organs functioning properly, including your brain.

Water consumption must be relatively constant, since water loss is relatively constant. You lose water through perspiration, urination, defecation, even respiration. Even if you stay indoors, behind insulating walls, you still need to drink between 1.5 and 2 liters of water every day. Outdoor pursuits, especially in extremes of cold, can easily double or even triple your water requirements. To maintain adequate hydration, the water going in must at least equal the water going out.

Not all your water consumption has to be in the form of plain water. Some people prefer sports drinks, available in powdered form for easy packing. (Sports drinks also provide a carbohydrate boost, but you'll get all the energy you need if you eat regularly.) You also get some water from other sources: coffee, tea, soup, fruit juice, and even a little from succulent foods. But to operate safely and at your best in winter, it's best to stay aware of your internal fluid level and drink ample amounts of water.

The water of winter tends to be a cold drink. This is not a problem: drinking cold water won't suddenly drop your body core temperature or otherwise predispose you to cold injury. Cool water may actually be absorbed by your body at a faster rate than warm water. Do not, however, eat snow, thinking that it will hydrate you. A mouthful of snow now and then won't hurt, but the energy required to melt snow in your mouth—for very little fluid—leaves you on the negative side of the hydration equation. The best use of a mouthful of snow is its cooling power when you're overheated from exertion.

Thirst ranks high as a sign that you need to drink, and many experts believe that the older you get, the more accurate the thirst indicator is. Even better in the cold outdoors is drinking enough water to prevent thirst. A strong need to drink, in fact, usually indicates that you're already

NOLS TIP

Check Urine Color

Establish a designated urination site at camp, and check the color of the snow after people have urinated. You may notice that someone has dark urine and encourage that person to stay better hydrated. You can also check yourself, comparing your urine color to that of others. You may, in fact, choose to utilize separate spots so you can monitor each individual's urine color.

into the early stages of dehydration. Despite the bother of having to stop regularly to urinate (while wearing layers of cold-weather clothing), frequent urination is a sign of adequate hydration. In most cases, clear or light yellow urine indicates adequate hydration. The darker your urine, the more dehydrated your body.

An adequately hydrated winter traveler is a disciplined drinker of water. Train yourself to drink a liter of water at the start of each day, and more with snacks and meals. Perhaps most importantly, discipline yourself to down a few gulps regularly throughout the day, especially when you're exercising. "Regularly" here means at least a couple of times an hour. Since you can consume water faster than your body can absorb water, it's better to drink frequently—say, a third of a liter every twenty minutes while exercising hard—than to gulp down a large volume of water infrequently. As long as you are snacking often—not a bad idea in the cold—you can't drink too much water.

> **N O L S   T I P**
>
> **Make Drinking Easy**
>
> *If you have to drop your pack and dig out your water bottle every time you want a drink, you increase the risk of not getting enough water. Carry a liter bottle in an insulated cover with a zip top and an integral loop. Keep the insulated water bottle clipped where you can reach it easily.*

WINTER WATER SOURCES

Subfreezing temperatures present an immediate problem for winter campers: natural water sources may become natural ice sources instead. Finding water in liquid form, either running or pooling, is a great reason to camp in a certain spot, or at least to stop and fill your water containers. It's easier and faster than melting snow, and it conserves petroleum products by saving you the burden of carrying extra fuel. Some streams are year-round sources of running water. Intermittent streams are usually dry or frozen in winter. Lakes are always liquid somewhere underneath the snow and ice. So, in the depths of winter, you'll need to carry a tool for breaking through ice to

reach water. You can use an ice ax, but a good ice chisel is easier and faster. In early winter, you may find open water or thin
ice at the inlets or outlets of lakes. In late winter, many frozen
lakes have "overflow" on them—water on the surface that has
seeped up from cracks in the old ice.

Taking water from a natural source in winter creates the
potential for injury. You might slip, slide, or otherwise fall in.
When streamside snowbanks are deep, dig into the snow to
install a ramp to the water's edge. The ramp makes getting
water safer and easier. Don't venture onto the surface of
frozen lakes or rivers without a considerable amount of dis-
criminating caution.

Melting Snow

Melting snow for water—always time-consuming and fuel-
inefficient—is often your only option. There are bad ways and
good ways to do it, however. Bad ways scorch the snow (actually the dust and other particulate matter in the snow), the
pot, or both, and the taste of the water you make is startlingly
unappealing. A good way is to start with a little water in the
pot (using a large pot saves time). If you have no water at all,
start with a little snow in the pot and stir it rapidly, over low
heat, until it melts. Then add snow as
it fits. Putting a lid on the pot speeds
up the melting process. A small shovel
makes your "water factory" more efficient, but you can also scoop snow
with pots, your gloved hands, or whatever works. Soft, fluffy snow is beautiful but low in water content. Heavy,
dense, icy snow has the most water.

It's a good idea to make sufficient
water for the evening, plus enough to
get started the next morning. In fact,
it's wise to make all the water you
can store before going to bed at night, filling your pots
and water bottles. It's inefficient to make water in the morn-

> **NOLS TIP**
>
> ### Double Your Snow-Melting
>
> When melting snow, place a second pot, also full of snow, on the lid of the pot already on the stove. The heat from the bottom pot will begin to melt the snow in the top pot.

ing. Besides, a winter evening is almost always warmer than a winter dawn.

You don't need to disinfect melted snow, if you choose your snow with care. Avoid any color but white, and pay attention—as you dig down into clean snow, you might hit a dirty layer.

Storing Water

A second challenge faced by winter campers is keeping water warm enough to stay a fluid. Some people sleep with their water bottles. This is fine, as long as the lids are screwed on tightly. If it's not screaming cold, a well-insulated bottle of water will not freeze in your tent at night.

Water can also be stored in camp by burying containers in snow. Use wide-mouthed containers, since those with narrow mouths freeze up faster and thaw more slowly. Snow is a wonderful insulator: under a foot of snow, a pot of water will remain mostly unfrozen, even if the temperature dips to minus 40. Take care to seal the hole well with snow to keep cold air out. Store water bottles with the top down, so that if a bit of ice forms on the top—which is now the bottom—the bottles will not be frozen shut. Mark the burial site, just in case it snows.

THAWING A FROZEN WATER BOTTLE

It takes about an hour to thaw a liter water bottle that has frozen solid. Therefore, the best advice is to do everything necessary to prevent your water bottle from freezing. If you fail, follow these directions:

1. Place the frozen water bottle upside down in a pot of boiling water until you can get the lid off.
2. Remove the lid and pour a little hot water into the bottle.
3. When a little ice has melted, pour that water into the pot to reheat.
4. Repeat the process until the ice is gone.
5. Use the hot water in the pot to make hot drinks.

Any insulation, even just a little, extends the time water will stay a fluid. Water placed near your body inside your pack usually gets enough heat from you to prevent freezing. Storing water in your pack wrapped in extra clothing, especially a good insulator such as fleece, gives you a lot more time before freezing starts—the exact amount of time depends on the ambient air temperature.

Disinfecting Water

Although clean melted snow is generally considered safe to drink, water from other sources should be disinfected. There are three proven ways to disinfect winter water.

Boiling. The rule is simple: once water is hot enough to produce one rolling bubble, it is free of organisms that can cause illness. Remember to use a lid for the pot: lids shorten boiling time and thus reduce fuel expenditure.

Filtration. Water filters physically strain out some of the organisms in water that can cause disease. The effectiveness of filters varies greatly; some remove only relatively large particles, and others remove virtually everything removable. Viruses are too small to be filtered out, but some filters kill viruses with iodine as the water passes through. Filtered water looks clean, but its quality depends on the specific filter. On the downside for winter travelers, filters freeze rather easily, and the expansion of freezing water within a filter may crack the unit, making it useless—problems that keep filters off most winter expeditions.

Halogenation. The chemicals chlorine and iodine, called halogens, are effective at killing waterborne pathogens, given enough of the chemical and enough time. Halogens are quickly and uselessly absorbed by anything organic in the water, such as sugar or leaf debris. Halogenation is affected by the pH and turbidity of the water and by the water temperature. It may take twice as long for halogens to work in icy water. Halogenation is generally more convenient and faster than boiling. On the negative side, halogens are not effective against a common pathogen, *Cryptosporidium*. Halogens also leave the water tasting bad, but this can be fixed by adding flavoring (such as energy drink powders) *after* disinfection is complete. If you flavor the water beforehand, the added substances may disrupt the disinfection process. All things considered, halogenation is the best choice on most winter expeditions.

FOOD AND NUTRITION

The value of food—as a source of power and warmth—is measured by its nutritional value. Nutrition is a somewhat imprecise science, but everyone agrees that a shortage of nutrients can cause energy slumps that bring early fatigue, lassitude, mind-numbness, and a predisposition for injury. Start every winter trip by planning to eat a nutritionally sound diet, balancing the best foods with what is practical to carry into the wild.

The most important element of good nutrition is water, as discussed earlier. Beyond this, there are three sources of energizing foods: carbohydrates, fats, and, to some extent, proteins. Although all foods must be digested into simple compounds before they can be burned for power, carbohydrates (sugars and starches) are digested most quickly and easily. Simple carbohydrates (simple sugars, such as granulated sugar, brown sugar,

N O L S   T I P

Use Bulk Rationing

At NOLS, a bulk rationing method is used to calculate how much food will be needed for an expedition. Careful bulk rationing provides adequate nutrition while minimizing pack weight. With the NOLS system, you figure out how much food (in pounds) you'll need per person per day, then multiply that number by the number of people and the number of days. If you'll be skiing (or hiking) with a full pack, perhaps pulling a sled, and the temperature is expected to stay cold, you'll want 2 to 2.25 pounds of food per person per day. That provides approximately 3,500 to 4,500 calories per person per day. If you expect extremely cold air and strenuous exertion, you may choose to pack 2.5 pounds per person per day, with a value of 4,000 to 5,000 calories per person per day. As an example, three people headed out for ten days of extremely strenuous skiing in subfreezing temperatures would pack 75 pounds of food (3 x 10 x 2.5).

honey, and molasses) are small molecular units that break down very fast, entering the bloodstream soon after you eat them. You get an energy boost right away, but most sugars are burned so quickly that energy levels can suddenly fall below your starting point if all you eat is simple carbohydrates. Therefore, complex carbohydrates (strings of simple sugars called starches, such as pasta, grains, fruits, and starchy vegetables) need to be a major portion of your winter diet. Being a more complex molecular unit, starches break down more slowly, providing power for the long haul. Simple sugars, in other words, are like kindling for a fire, and starches are the big, fat logs.

Fat is so important that your body will manufacture it from carbohydrates and proteins if you run short. Fats (cheese, nuts, butter, peanut butter, meat) break down very slowly in the digestive process, so more time is required for them to provide energy. That's a good thing when you need a steady source of energy over an extended period, such as long nights in the sleeping bag. But if you're used to eating a low-fat diet, add fats slowly to allow your digestive system to adjust.

Proteins are made up of amino acids, and amino acids are the basic substance of human tissue. Proteins (meat, milk products, eggs, cheese, seeds, nuts, whole grains) are not a primary energy source, but your body will use them if nothing else is available or if you exercise for a long time. But because tissue is continually lost and replaced (and new tissue is built after you exercise), proteins are essential. All the amino acids are synthesized by your body, except for eight, which have to be eaten. A "complete protein" has all eight of these amino acids.

If you eat a variety of foods from all three sources, and enough of it, you'll get not only the nutrition you need but also the vitamins and minerals necessary for health and performance in the cold. For more information, consult the *NOLS Nutrition Field Guide* (see Resources).

Here are some more tips for planning your winter menu:

- Apart from basic nutrition, the single most important factor in cold-weather food consumption is eating food you enjoy.

BASIC FOOD CHECKLIST

Breakfast
- [ ] Oatmeal
- [ ] Cream of Rice or Wheat
- [ ] Hash-brown potatoes
- [ ] Granola
- [ ] Pancake mix

Lunch
- [ ] Bagels
- [ ] Cheese
- [ ] Nuts and seeds
- [ ] Dried fruit
- [ ] Crackers
- [ ] Energy bars
- [ ] Candy
- [ ] Trail mix

Dinner
- [ ] Cheese
- [ ] Pasta
- [ ] Rice
- [ ] Tortillas

- [ ] Couscous
- [ ] Hummus
- [ ] Bulgur
- [ ] Instant potato pearls
- [ ] Pepperoni, sliced
- [ ] Bacon (save the grease for cooking)
- [ ] Beef jerky
- [ ] Hot drinks
- [ ] Cocoa
- [ ] Tang
- [ ] Jell-O
- [ ] Tea
- [ ] Coffee
- [ ] Instant soups
- [ ] Butter
- [ ] Olive oil
- [ ] Powdered milk
- [ ] Salsa
- [ ] Sugar, brown
- [ ] Spices

- Your cold tolerance will improve if you eat a high-fat snack (about one-third of the calories from fat) every couple of hours. In fact, your blood sugar will stay sufficiently high if you eat a full breakfast and a full dinner and snack throughout the day's activities. Food and drink every hour helps to maintain warmth and strength. Another snack just before bedtime will help keep you warm while you sleep.

- Spoilage is not a problem on winter trips, because the cold temperature preserves the food. The biggest problem will be keeping food unfrozen. Wrap the food bag in your pack inside extra clothing for insulation. Keep snacks handy (and thawed) in a pocket near your body.

- Cut your cheese, meats, and butter into chunks before leaving home. Even if they freeze solid, you will still have manageable pieces.

- Think simple. You'll be cold and tired, so quick, one-pot meals will be more appealing. For recipes and abundant information on food and nutrition, consult *NOLS Cookery* (see Resources).

COOKING IN THE COLD

Cooking in winter takes much more time and fuel than it does in summer—partly due to the colder air, and partly due to the fact that you might be melting snow for most of your water. Whether you construct an elaborate snow kitchen (see chapter 9) or simply fire up the stove in the lee of your tent, here are some guidelines:

- Cook in the open. Although you can, with adequate ventilation, cook in the vestibule of a tent or under a tarp, deadly carbon monoxide can build up quickly in an enclosed space, so cooking in the open is strongly recommended.
- Use a stove pad to keep the stove from melting into the snow underneath (see chapter 3), and use pot pads (pieces of closed-cell foam work well) to avoid setting pots directly in the snow. (If you do set a pot in the snow, remember to brush the snow off the bottom before setting the pot back on the stove, or risk extinguishing your stove.)
- Warm, dry lighters work much better than cold, wet ones, so keep several spares in your clothes pockets, where they'll be warm, dry, and easy to find. Electric lighters are more reliable than flint lighters.
- Conserve as much fuel as possible by using windscreens, windbreaks, and reflector shields for the stove; using lids for pots; and never letting a pot of water reach a full, rolling boil.
- Don't let the stove get icy overnight or between meals. Keep it well covered, preferably in a bag, when you're not using it.

- Be very careful when refilling the stove. Wear light gloves, because the evaporation of fuel from your skin can cause frostbite.
- Keep your kitchen well organized to prevent time-wasting searches for small items lost in the snow.

FOOD-RELATED HYGIENE

Mealtime creates the greatest opportunity for germs to be passed around a group. Stomach complaints are the most common medical problem on expeditions, and they are almost always the result of bad hygiene. Although the cold of winter reduces the opportunity, thoughtful attention to limiting the trading of germs remains important.

Wash your hands prior to meal preparation. Clean hands are the single most important factor in stopping the spread of germs. You can get your hands relatively germ-free with a little bit of water and an antibacterial soap. When water is in short supply, you can use a hand sanitizer, preferably one with alcohol; this type works best against germs and probably won't freeze. But remember, skin wet with alcohol can get frostbitten quickly.

Periodic washing of kitchen gear is also a good idea, but as long as the temperature stays below 38 degrees F, your gear will remain relatively germ-free if you allow it to cool off

---

BASIC KITCHEN GEAR CHECKLIST

☐ Food
☐ Large insulated mug
☐ Small bowl with snap-on lid (to store leftovers)
☐ Spoon, for eating
☐ Large spoon, for cooking
☐ Spatula
☐ Pots
☐ Frying pan
☐ Channel locks (angled pliers) with insulated handles, for pot-gripping

rapidly and if you bring your next meal to the boiling point during preparation. Likewise, leftovers will remain safe if they are allowed to cool quickly; before eating them, return them to high heat in boiling water.

Good hygiene also dictates that contact between individuals be limited at mealtime. Don't share water bottles, cups, or personal utensils, and don't reach into group food bags for a handful of trail mix—instead, pour the food out into your hand.

Chapter 8

Winter Health

When you're used to being warm, both physiologically and psychologically, the cold feels colder. Although this may make you more susceptible to cold injuries, such as hypothermia and frostbite, there are thoughtful and appropriate things you can do to stay healthy, even in extremes of cold. This is not necessarily difficult to do, but it does require knowledge and discipline. Although you will adapt to the cold, you must always pay close attention to your body's well-being, especially in winter.

ADAPTATION TO COLD

Humans who have lived for centuries, years, months, or even weeks in cold climates adapt to the cold. These adaptations fall into two categories: physiological and psychological.

When compared with heat-related adaptations, we, as a species, haven't done much physiologically to adapt to cold. Such evolutionary changes take a long time. But even on a winter expedition of two to three weeks, your physiological changes will likely be measurable (should you have the means to do so).

These changes take several forms. One is an increase in your basal metabolic rate. That is, more calories are burned at rest to produce more heat. This change might take some time, but an immediate bodily response to cold is to burn whatever is available to make heat. To the winter traveler, this means eating more, or at least enough, to stay warm. Another change is that the periphery of the body, the part nearest the cold, begins to maintain itself at a lower temperature, and shivering starts to occur at a lower temperature. Capillaries open up more readily to send warm blood to cold extremities. You may have experienced this phenomenon to some degree already. For example, your hands get cold—uncomfortably or even painfully cold— and then as your capillaries open up, often with exercise, your hands get warm again. Over time, your body learns to respond to cold with cold-induced vasodilatation more immediately. In the meantime, you need to keep your extremities warm by covering them with adequate insulation.

Finally, the amount of fat near the surface (subcutaneous fat) and around vital organs begins to increase. Health-wise, however, there's no good reason to gain weight before a winter expedition, but there's no good reason to lose weight either—unless, of course, you're obese.

Mental tolerance for cold, or psychological adaptation, is an elusive but important aspect of dealing with winter. This change appears to begin almost immediately, and it continues with prolonged exposure. After a while, the cold doesn't feel as cold. In the words of Dr. Murray Hamlet, former Director of

---

TRAINING FOR COLD AND HEAT

You can get mighty hot skiing on a cold day, so it's not a bad idea to train for heat and cold at the same time. You acclimate to the cold by being out in it. To train for heat, you need to exercise in the heat. Any activity that makes you hot enough to sweat profusely (for example, running while overdressed) will teach your body to unload excess heat via sweating. In other words, you can learn to perspire efficiently. If you take an extended winter trip after adapting to exercise in the heat, you will perform better overall when you exercise strenuously in the cold. (Keep in mind, however, that when skiing a frozen landscape, you want to limit your actual sweating to a minimum.)

Operations at the U.S. Army Research Institute for Environmental Medicine and the "guru of cold," one learns "to be miserable." But a gray area exists between accepting the cold and staying safe in the cold. You must still deal proactively with the physiological stresses of winter.

WINTER WELLNESS
There are many habits you can develop to better deal with extreme cold. The first and foremost is maintenance of general health: a well-nourished, rested, and generally healthy person almost always deals with cold, or other stressors, better than someone who is less healthy.

The most important factor in maintaining winter health is to stay adequately hydrated: again, be sure to drink enough water. You also need to eat well. The energy you require to move, stay warm, and enjoy yourself comes from the food you digest. In addition, make sure you dress correctly, in appropriate layers, to maintain body heat and reduce exertion.

It is important to stay in shape. Fit people wear down more slowly than the unfit do. They stay more alert and more coordinated. Train for enduring the long, cold haul before you actually attempt it. Once you're out on an expedition, take rest days, and mix days of light exercise with more strenuous days. Rest allows your body to repair tissue. It also lets your body systems recharge, which is especially important: white blood cells, to take one example, dwindle in number, sometimes significantly, after only two days of stress without adequate rest. On days of strenuous exercise, take care of chores quickly, and take some time to relax. Fatigue makes you susceptible to bad decisions and a poor disposition.

Finally, think positively and make the most of a given situation. There's a famous story in which a Zen monk falls from a cliff and grabs a blueberry bush on the way down to stop his fall. As the roots begin to rip from the cliff wall, realizing his imminent doom, he notices a ripe blueberry clinging to the bush, reaches out, and eats it. Making the best of every situation is not an ability we are all born with, but it is a habit we can all develop. Nothing makes or breaks an expedition—health-wise and otherwise—more predictably than attitude.

Besides being in good health, when you step into the wilderness, you should carry the knowledge and skills to recognize, treat, and prevent illness and injury. You should, in other words, be trained in wilderness medicine. The standard training for leaders at NOLS is the Wilderness First Responder course, an eighty-hour curriculum with a twenty-four-hour biannual refresher (see Resources).

HYPOTHERMIA

A drop in the normal temperature of the body's core—hypothermia—subtly steals one's ability to make rational decisions and may be related to other winter injuries and illnesses. Winter travelers need to be well-educated about hypothermia and self-aware enough to monitor themselves.

Hypothermia is a progressive problem, one that carries you deeper and deeper into trouble. In addition to growing less rational, the signs of hypothermia include a set of indications called the "umbles": Gross coordination is lost, and you begin to *stumble*. With a brain dulled by the cold, you begin to *fumble* with gear and clothing, *mumble* instead of speaking clearly, and *grumble*, sometimes apathetically, about life, the universe, and everything.

If a victim's core temperature continues to drop, uncontrollable shivering starts. Shivering produces heat, but it requires high energy output. If heat isn't trapped near the body or energy replenished with food, the core temperature continues to drop ever faster. Eventually, if hypothermia goes untreated, shivering stops and the victim enters what may be termed a "metabolic icebox": the body grows progressively more rigid and colder to the touch, the pulse slows and weakens, and respiration may become impossible to detect. Although a person can survive for hours, perhaps days, in this deteriorating condition, the eventual outcome is death unless quality care is provided.

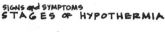

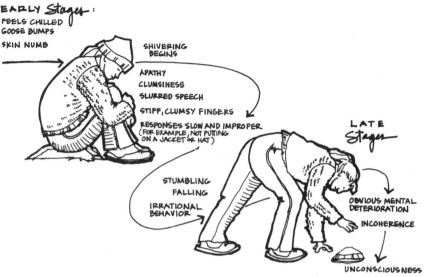

SIGNS and SYMPTOMS
STAGES of HYPOTHERMIA

EARLY *Stages*:
FEELS CHILLED
GOOSE BUMPS
SKIN NUMB
SHIVERING BEGINS
APATHY
CLUMSINESS
SLURRED SPEECH
STIFF, CLUMSY FINGERS
RESPONSES SLOW AND IMPROPER (FOR EXAMPLE, NOT PUTTING ON A JACKET OR HAT)

LATE *Stages*
STUMBLING
FALLING
IRRATIONAL BEHAVIOR
OBVIOUS MENTAL DETERIORATION
INCOHERENCE
UNCONSCIOUSNESS

For management purposes, hypothermia can be divided into two categories: mild and severe. A patient with mild hypothermia is trying to warm up internally and can still talk, eat, and shiver. The environment must be altered so that the heat being produced internally is not lost. Get the patient out of wet clothes and into something dry, and out of the wind and cold and into some kind of shelter, even if the only thing available is waterproof or windproof clothing. Cover the patient's head and neck, where critical heat is easily lost. If the patient can eat and drink, provide simple carbohydrates to stoke the inner fire. Fluids are more important than solids; a warm (not hot), sweet drink will add a tiny bit of heat and a lot of simple sugar for energy. Even cold fluids are better than no fluids. If the patient can still exercise, keep him or her moving after initial treatment. If the patient can't exercise, do all you can to encourage the entrapment of inner heat production—insulate the patient from the ground; bundle him or her in dry insulation; have the patient snuggle with warm people;

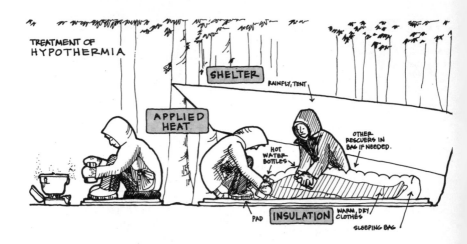

TREATMENT OF HYPOTHERMIA

SHELTER — RAINFLY, TENT

APPLIED HEAT

HOT WATER BOTTLES

OTHER RESCUERS IN BAG IF NEEDED.

PAD   INSULATION   WARM, DRY CLOTHES

SLEEPING BAG

place hot water bottles in the hands, at the feet, and in the armpits and groin (but not against naked skin)—and wait until the patient returns to normal. Forget about taking the person's temperature: other more obvious signs and symptoms will allow you to assess what really matters.

A patient with severe hypothermia is semiconscious or unconscious and has stopped shivering. The ability to warm up has been lost. Handle such a patient gently—roughness can overload a cold heart and stop it. Remove clothing and bundle the patient up in as much dry insulation as possible, well insulated from the ground. Wrap hot water bottles or heat packs in dry socks or shirts and place them appropriately: palms of hands, soles of feet, armpits, groin. Finish with a vapor barrier—a tent fly, sheet of plastic, garbage bags—anything to trap whatever heat is still left in the body. The final product is a cocoon, a "hypothermia wrap," open only at the mouth and nose. Do not try to force food or drink. Go for help. You should treat for severe hypothermia even if the patient appears to be dead. No patient is dead, as far as you're concerned, unless he or she is warm and dead.

The best strategy, however, is to prevent hypothermia in the first place. Follow this advice:

- Wear clothing that retains body heat, even when wet (no cotton).
- Stay dry by wearing layers of clothing; remove them before sweating starts, and add them before chilling occurs.
- Drink lots of water.
- Eat a lot of food, especially carbohydrates.
- Maintain a pace that prevents overexertion, and rest often.
- In a group, watch one another for signs of hypothermia. Treat it early, and if one person needs treatment, play it safe and warm everyone up.

FROSTBITE

Frostbite is the localized freezing of tissue, and it often goes hand in hand with hypothermia. Proper treatment of frostbite can save near-frozen tissue and reduce the damage to already frozen tissue.

As with hypothermia, frostbite is progressive. It starts as a superficial problem, with no actual freezing of tissue. Initially, skin is pale and numb, cold to the touch. If you notice it, treat it immediately with passive skin-to-skin contact: cover a nose with your warm hand, stick a cold hand against your warm stomach, or put cold toes against the warm abdomen of a friend. Don't rub the cold skin, and don't place it near a hot heat source, because numb tissue is very susceptible to heat injury. The skin should soon return to normal.

Untreated, the condition progresses to partial-thickness frostbite (partially frozen tissue), indicated by pale, numb, cold skin. The skin moves when you gently press on it. This problem looks superficial, and you may not know whether it's true frostbite until the skin is warmed. Passive warming should begin immediately. Give ibuprofen, if available, and lots of water to drink. If blisters form after warming, you know that the problem was partial-thickness frostbite, and a physician should be consulted as soon as possible. In the meantime, do two things: (1) Leave the blister bubble intact; it protects the underlying tissue and lessens the chance for infection. (2) Be careful to prevent refreezing. Blisters can refreeze quickly, multiplying the damage.

Skin with full-thickness frostbite is pale, numb, and hard—unmoving to gentle touch. Normal field conditions make the warming of deep frostbite impractical. Often, all you can do is remove the clothing from the frostbitten part (unless it's frozen to the skin), gently bundle the frozen skin in lots of dry insulation, and evacuate the patient. If refreezing is unlikely, however, and you have the means available, full-thickness frostbite is best treated by rapid warming in water of approximately 104 to 108 degrees F (40 to 42 degrees C). Water that is too hot can cause heat damage, and water that is too cold delays warming. Warming is usually accomplished in thirty to forty minutes, but it's better to err on the side of caution and warm longer than necessary. Soft, dry cotton should be placed between thawed digits; otherwise, contact with the frostbitten skin should be avoided. Pain is often intense, and painkillers should be given when available, before thawing. Ibuprofen started as soon as possible seems to reduce the extent of tissue damage. Keep the patient well-hydrated, and prevent refreezing. Find a doctor as soon as possible.

To prevent frostbite, follow the same guidelines for preventing hypothermia. In addition, wear appropriate clothing; avoid snug clothing that restricts circulation, especially on the feet and hands. Take care to protect your skin from wind and from contact with cold metal and gasoline. Avoid alcohol and tobacco, which can impair blood flow. If your toes start to hurt from the cold, rejoice that the nerves are functional, and stop and warm them to prevent permanent injury.

NONFREEZING COLD INJURY

Nonfreezing cold injury (NFCI), also known as immersion foot or trenchfoot, is a cold-weather emergency resulting from prolonged contact with cold—and usually moisture—which causes inadequate circulation and results in tissue damage. The foot first shows a bit of swelling and discoloration (usually white or bluish), and the patient may complain of numbness. This may be

the only sign, unless the damage is substantial. Then, on warming, the foot swells extensively with excess fluid, and the damaged tissue typically looks red. The patient may complain of
tingling pain, often severe, that doesn't let up. Blisters may form,
followed by ulcers where the blisters have fallen off, revealing
dead tissue underneath. In severe cases, gangrene may result.

If you think that you or a companion is developing NFCI,
warm the foot in warm water (as for frostbite), then carefully
dry it. You can also keep the foot elevated above the level of the
heart while you gently warm it with passive skin-to-skin contact. If the foot looks dirty, carefully wash it before drying it. Do
not rub the foot or place it near a strong heat source, such as a
fire or stove, both of which can damage the tissue. Start the
patient on a regimen of over-the-counter anti-inflammatory
drugs (aspirin or, even better, ibuprofen), following the label
directions. Keep the patient in dry socks at all times. It will probably take twenty-four to forty-eight hours before the severity of
the damage is fully apparent. If the foot is hurting or obviously
swollen or develops blisters, get the patient to a physician.

NFCI is encouraged by poor nutrition, dehydration, wet
socks, inadequate clothing, and the constriction of blood flow
by too-tight boots and socks. Make sure that your boots fit,
with plenty of room for your socks, and keep a dry pair of
socks on hand at all times (preferably packed in a plastic bag).
People who sweat heavily are also more susceptible to NFCI,
and an antiperspirant spray can reduce sweating and thus
reduce the risk. Periodically, preferably twice a day, dry your
feet and gently massage them before stuffing them back into
your boots. Do not sleep in wet socks.

Once you have suffered NFCI, it can recur after a shorter
exposure to cold, wet conditions. The damage is cumulative,
and tends to grow worse with each repetition, along with the
possibility of permanent consequences.

SOLAR RADIATION INJURY
The sun, our bright source of light and life, can also be a
source of medical problems. Sunshine strikes the earth in rays

of varying wavelengths. Long rays, or infrared radiation, are unseen but are felt as heat. Intermediate-length rays are visible as light. Shorter rays, or ultraviolet (UV) radiation, are also invisible and are divided into three types: (1) ultraviolet A (UVA), which is beneficial in low doses but increases the risk of skin cancer in high doses; (2) UVB, which is primarily responsible for sunburn and skin cancer; and (3) UVC, the shortest and most dangerous, which is reflected or absorbed by the ozone layer. UV rays contain enough energy to damage DNA in living skin and eye cells, which affects the cells' ability to heal and reproduce. UV radiation is of particular concern to the winter camper, as reflection from snow and ice can increase the damage it causes.

Sunburn
The earliest sign of skin damage is a radiation burn caused by UV light: sunburn. Skin becomes red, painful, sometimes slightly swollen, and, in the worst case, blistered. Cool compresses provide relief. Moisturizing lotions and creams, including aloe, help, as does ibuprofen for pain and swelling. The patient should be kept well hydrated.

Sunburns are preventable. Tightly woven clothing blocks a large amount of UV radiation, especially if it stays reasonably dry. A full-brimmed hat shades your head and neck, and a floppy brim breaks up scattered UV rays better than a rigid brim does. A bandanna hanging down behind a baseball cap can also protect your neck, if the cold does not demand a warmer head covering. Sunscreens with a sun protection factor (SPF) of 15 are sufficient for most skin types. Higher SPFs provide more protection, but the degree of protection is not comparable to the numbers. For instance, SPF 30 is not twice as effective as SPF 15. There is probably no reason to choose an SPF higher than 30, but make sure that the sunscreen you choose protects against both UVA and UVB. Sunscreens are maximally effective when applied to warm skin and allowed to soak in for about thirty minutes before exposure. People with very susceptible skin types might be better off blocking

UV radiation completely with an opaque substance such as zinc oxide on exposed skin. Lips require constant attention. Be sure to carry and use a lip balm with a SPF of at least 15. The moisturizing effect of the balm also prevents cracked lips, a common problem in the dry air of winter.

Snow Blindness

Eyes are especially vulnerable to UV rays reflected off snow, and six to twelve hours after overexposure, the eyes may begin to hurt, as if they are full of sand. The patient often complains of blurred vision, and the eyes may look red and swollen. The cornea of the eye has been sunburned, making it very sensitive to light. Although the condition is called snow blindness, the patient is not truly blind—merely practically so, because it hurts so much to open the eyes. Cool, wet compresses can be applied for pain, and a small amount of an ophthalmic ointment can be applied several times a day for two to three days. To apply the ointment, pull down the bottom lid of the eye and insert a thin line of ointment; have the patient blink a few times and then keep the eyes shut until the ointment melts. If possible, remain in camp and allow the patient to rest his or her eyes for twenty-four hours, during which time exposure to UV light should be avoided. Snow blindness almost always resolves harmlessly in a day or two. If the problem doesn't resolve, a visit to a doctor is warranted.

Snow blindness can be prevented by wearing well-fitting sunglasses that block all UV light. On snow or water, sunglasses should have side shields or a wrap-around design to block reflected light. Shields can be improvised from tape.

Sun Bumps

Some light-sensitive people develop small pimples or blisters after exposure to UV radiation. They're common on snow, at high altitudes, under clouds, and when it's warm enough to walk around with uncovered skin, but they can occur under other conditions as well. The skin often swells and reddens, and it may itch. The hands and face, typically receiving the most UV exposure, are most likely to develop sun bumps. The bumps usually appear one to four days after initial exposure and take about two weeks to go away. The best guess by experts is that sun bumps are an allergic reaction to UVA. Protect the patient, and prevent the problem as you would for sunburn. Antihistamines may provide some relief.

ALTITUDE ILLNESS

High above sea level, it's nearly always cold. In such places, you enter a realm where illnesses specific to high altitude may occur. These problems result from hypoxia—insufficient oxygen in the blood for normal tissue function—a result of the ever-decreasing barometric pressure as you ascend. Altitude illnesses affect the brain, the lungs, or both. These illnesses—which range in severity from mild to fatal—are influenced by four factors: (1) how high you go, (2) how fast you gain altitude, (3) the altitude at which you sleep, and (4) predisposing factors, such as genetics and differences in individual physiology, which are not well understood.

ACCLIMATIZATION

The rate of acclimatization—the process of physiologically adjusting to high altitude—differs based on individual physiology and the altitude attained, but almost everyone can acclimatize, given enough time. Most people adjust well enough to prevent illness if they spend two to three days in the 8,000 to 12,000-foot range and gain no more than 1,000 feet of sleeping altitude each successive day. So if you slept at 14,000 feet last night, you can climb beyond 15,000 feet today, but you should drop back down to no more than approximately 15,000 feet to sleep. Adequate hydration and nutrition are also significant factors in acclimatization.

Acute Mountain Sickness and High-Altitude Cerebral Edema

Acute mountain sickness (AMS) is the most common altitude illness. Symptoms of AMS usually appear within six to ten hours of arrival at altitude, but they can appear in as little as one hour. The symptoms range in severity from mild to moderate. Headache is usually the first and by far the most common complaint. Other symptoms include anorexia (loss of appetite), nausea and vomiting, insomnia (inability to sleep), lassitude (weariness, exhaustion), dizziness, and unusual fatigue. Those affected by AMS are typically short of breath while exercising, but breathing quickly returns to normal with rest. AMS does not cause physiological damage, but it does indicate that you are not acclimatized to a specific altitude. Since it's impossible to predict who will progress from mild to severe illness, you must stop ascending until the symptoms disappear. Rest may be the only treatment needed. Otherwise, ibuprofen often alleviates the headache. Light exercise, and the resulting increase in breathing, may relieve mild symptoms of AMS. Supplemental oxygen, however, is the drug of choice for more serious problems. Acetazolamide is a prescription drug that speeds the resolution of mild to moderate AMS in about three-quarters of patients, but it may take up to twenty-four hours to work. If you are treated successfully with drugs for mild to moderate AMS, you can continue to ascend. If the symptoms do not resolve within twenty-four to forty-eight hours, you must descend.

If the symptoms of AMS don't improve, it could indicate that you are developing high-altitude cerebral edema (HACE), a serious condition with a high risk of death. With HACE, fluid leaks out of capillaries and collects around the brain, which can be injured by the increasing pressure.

HACE develops progressively over hours to days. It can cause ataxia (loss of coordination) that, when severe, could make even sitting up impossible. HACE also results in a dramatically altered mental status, including disorientation, irritability, combativeness, personality changes, or hallucinations. A severe headache is common—a constant throbbing that is unrelieved by rest or medication. Lethargy, weakness, and vomiting are also common.

Descent is absolutely critical if HACE is the problem. Descending as little as 1,500 feet can bring favorable results.

Dexamethasone, a steroid, can reduce pressure on the brain, producing results in about twelve hours. Acetazolamide can also be helpful. Note that drugs, including oxygen, should never be used as a substitute for descent.

If descent is delayed, in addition to drugs, a person with HACE may benefit greatly from being placed in a portable hyperbaric chamber (such as the Gamow bag). This device consists of an elongated bag made of sturdy nylon. Pressure inside the bag is increased by means of a simple foot pump, simulating a descent of up to several thousand feet relative to the actual altitude. The patient may benefit from the administration of supplemental oxygen while undergoing "descent" within the bag.

High-Altitude Pulmonary Edema

High-altitude pulmonary edema (HAPE) affects the lungs and is the most common form of severe altitude illness and thus the one most likely to cause death. HAPE typically begins on the second night of reaching a specific altitude and is uncommon beyond four days at a given altitude. The pressure in the pulmonary arteries rises, and fluid seeps out of the pulmonary capillaries and begins to fill the alveolar spaces. In essence, you drown.

The first symptoms are a decreased ability to exercise and a dry cough. Shortness of breath unrelieved by rest then develops. Later in the illness, breathing is often accompanied by gurgling sounds audible to the naked ear. As fluid continues to collect in the lungs, a productive cough develops, eventually producing a frothy sputum that is pink from blood. Chest pain can be expected.

HAPE requires immediate descent. Descent should not cause overexertion, however, because exercise may increase pulmonary pressure and make the problem worse. Supplemental oxygen can reduce pulmonary arterial pressure 30% to 50%, enough to possibly reverse the illness. Patients who can sit should do so, because this usually decreases respiratory distress by allowing fluid in the lungs to settle, via gravity, in the lower portions.

If descent is delayed, a portable hyperbaric chamber may be of great benefit. Nifedipine, a drug that reduces blood pressure in the pulmonary system, can be given according to pre-arranged instructions from a physician, but this should be considered only when descent is delayed.

Preventing Altitude Illness
Staged ascent brings about acclimatization and is the best way to prevent altitude illness. Above 10,000 feet, most people should gain no more than 1,000 to 1,500 feet of sleeping altitude per twenty-four hours. Beyond this, adequate hydration is critical. Drink enough water to keep your urine clear and copious. A high-calorie diet is also essential. A diet of 70% or more carbohydrates may aid in the prevention of altitude illness, since carbs require less oxygen to metabolize than other foods do. A high-carbohydrate diet does not seem to help at altitudes below 16,000 to 17,000 feet, however. Avoid respiratory depressants, such as sleeping pills and alcohol, especially during the first two to three days at a specific altitude. Acetazolamide or dexamethasone can be taken prophylactically as prescribed by a doctor. Both drugs are effective in preventing AMS, but not HACE or HAPE.

Fitness does not protect against altitude illness. Physical fitness before ascent is a bonus, but training to prepare you physiologically for altitude must be done at altitude.

LESSER-KNOWN WINTER WORRIES
Hard exercise on a cold day, the kind of workout that requires aggressive panting, might lead to an unusual condition called frozen lung. Temperatures must be low, usually below 0 degrees F. No tissue actually freezes, but severe bronchial irritation results from sucking down very cold, dry air faster than the airway can warm and moisturize it. The irritation produces spasms in the muscles of the airway and a burning pain, with the possibility of coughing up blood. Increased mucus production frequently creates wheezing sounds when the sufferer breathes. A severe case can last one to two weeks. Treatment is

rest, warm and humidified air to breathe, and plenty of water to drink. Prevention is less painful: wear a hooded parka and a facemask, or breathe through a fluffy scarf.

A worrisome phenomenon, which can occur with temperatures as high as 60 degrees F, is chilblains, a condition consisting of red, itchy skin lesions. When skin that has been kept cool and moist for a long time is warmed, it causes a rush of blood to the heat-dilated vessels near the surface of the body. The swollen vessels can't take the load, so fluid and metabolic waste products leak out of the vessels and into the surrounding tissue. That tissue swells, itches, and hurts. Pus may fill the lesions in severe cases. Treatment includes keeping the damaged skin warm and dry and applying a protective ointment. Prevention is simple: keep your skin warm and dry.

As the icy tendrils of winter swirled around his house in 1862, Maurice Raynaud took pen in frigid hand to scratch out a description of the disease that would bear his name. Raynaud's syndrome results from intermittent spasms in the peripheral vessels of the fingers or toes and, occasionally, the ears and nose. Color changes accompany this painful response to cold—usually white, but sometimes red or blue. Nobody knows what causes Raynaud's syndrome, but thousands suffer from it with the slightest drop in temperature. Many treatments have been tried, including avoidance of cold (which ruins winter fun), tranquilizers, vasodilating drugs, hormones, and, in extreme cases, a sympathectomy (cutting the sympathetic nerves so the blood vessels can't constrict).

For the past decade, researchers at the U.S. Army Research Institute of Environmental Medicine in Natick, Massachusetts, have been experimenting with techniques to countercondition those with Raynaud's syndrome. Test subjects were required to keep their hands or feet in hot water for fifteen to twenty minutes while the rest of their bodies remained cold. Then, with hands or feet still in hot water, they were moved to a warm ambient environment for fifteen to twenty minutes. Eventually, the brain is conditioned to keep the peripheral vasculature open, without the hot water, despite the changing air temperature. The institute says that 90% of patients improve, and the conditioning may last for years before it has to be repeated.

Chapter 9

The Winter Camp

CAMPSITE SELECTION

One of the most rewarding parts of winter camping is getting to bed down at night in a well-made winter camp. If you're a camper—winter-wise or not—you already appreciate the value of choosing the perfect spot to set up camp. Beyond a great view in a peaceful place, "perfect" here means safe and comfortable. And in winter, fewer daylight hours mean longer nights, so you'll be spending more time in camp than you do in other seasons—and thus enjoying your choice of sites longer.

Safety considerations require a careful look around and up. If your campsite is anywhere beneath an avalanche slope, measure the alpha angle—the angle from your site to the highest avalanche starting zone above you. An alpha angle of twenty degrees or higher is too close for comfort. For hard glacial ice, use fifteen degrees. Also look out for "widowmakers," large dead limbs or whole dead trees that could fall from old age, a load of snow, a high wind, or some combination of factors. Camp away from cliff edges that someone might stumble off of, and avoid cliff bottoms, where sliding rocks or snow could come to rest.

Unless you're very confident of the weather forecast, you should also evaluate your campsite with respect to a storm. If a

NOLS TIP

Arrive Refreshed

When you're nearly ready to stop and set up camp, slow down your pace for the last fifteen to twenty minutes of skiing. A slower pace allows your clothing to shed some of the perspiration collected from your earlier exertions. Your body also benefits from a cool-down period, ridding itself of some of the by-products of hard exercise, such as lactic acid. Cooling down is important after any strenuous athletic activity, and few equal the effort of skiing with a heavy pack.

blizzard drops a load of snow, will you be able to leave your camp in safety? If nearby slopes, now lightly dusted with snow, become heavily laden, could they become avalanche-prone?

With deep snow cover, the choice of sites becomes, in some respects, easier. You don't need a flat spot, because you can make one. You don't need to avoid logs, roots, and rocks, because they're buried. You don't need a water source (although a source of liquid water is a major score), because you can melt snow.

Whether the landscape is frozen or not, avoiding human pollution of natural water sources must be a high priority. Winter camps must not leave trash, gear, food, or spilled fuel behind. The snow will eventually go away, but your garbage will remain. Set your camp at least 200 feet (about 70 adult paces) from springs, streams, rivers, ponds, and lakes. In some areas, out of a desperate need to preserve water quality and the overall quality of the wilderness experience, land managers have established regulations that require camps to be located an acceptable distance from water sources.

Wind, often a blessing on a bug-ridden summer day, tends to be a curse in winter. Gusty winds can rattle ice-stiffened tent walls throughout the night, keeping you awake. Wind-blown snow can bury the door of the tent, and it may find its way through the tiniest opening to drift across your bedroom. If the view from an open ridge is irresistible, hope for a calm night. Better yet, choose a site out of the wind or the possibility of wind. The lee side of a broad ridge may be a good choice, as long as you stay off slopes that could avalanche. A site behind natural windbreaks—a thick stand of trees, a large rock, a rise in the ground—is another possibility, but remember that windbreaks create natural snowdrifts roughly five times longer than the breaks are high. In the open, you can build a windbreak around your shelter.

Choose higher or lower campsites based on the weather and temperature. Calm, cold air sinks, keeping the upper end of a valley slightly warmer than the lower end. On blustery nights, however, higher ground may catch the wind and be colder than lower, protected sites. Always avoid the lowest ground in the area, such as a valley bottom, where the frosty air will settle overnight. If possible, select a site that will catch the early-morning sun, adding many degrees of joy to your own rising. Atop a knoll protected by trees is often an excellent spot.

> **N O L S   T I P**
>
> **Serve Hot Drinks**
>
> *As soon as you've chosen a campsite after a long day of travel, have someone set up a temporary kitchen, fire up the stove, and start melting snow and making hot drinks. The drinks will hydrate you, warm you a tiny bit, give you an energy boost (if they contain sugar), and uplift you mentally.*

TENTS

Unless the snowpack is unusually dense—dense enough to support your weight—you'll need to ski-pack a platform for your tent. Wearing your skis, walk back and forth over an area about twice the size of the "footprint" of the tent until the snow is firmly packed. The extra space compressed around the tent will come in handy: you can set up the tent more easily, since you won't have to wear your skis, and you'll have room to move around outside the tent without putting on your skis.

> **N O L S   T I P**
>
> **Set Up Early**
>
> *Begin setting up camp early, while you still have light. Trying to pitch a tent in the dark increases the risk not only of fatigue and short tempers but also of accidents and damage to both relationships and the environment.*

It's going to be an hour—more or less—before the snow platform sinters enough to walk on it without skis. Use this time to ski-pack a route to the latrine areas and a water source, and a platform for your snow kitchen.

Consider building a snow wall on the windward side of the tent as a windbreak, or all around the tent if the wind doesn't come steadily from one direction. For maximum effectiveness, the windbreak must be close to the tent. When the winds are severe and a sheltered spot is unobtainable, dig down into the snow a couple of feet before stomping out the tent platform. This will provide some protection from the wind while you're building the platform and more protection for the tent.

Pitch your tent with a low end toward the wind and the door at a ninety-degree angle to the wind, if possible. High wind or a snow load can put tremendous pressure on the nylon, so

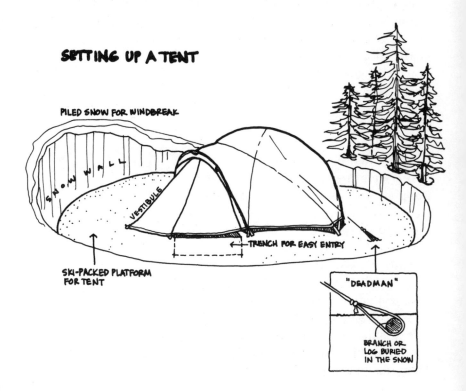

SETTING UP A TENT

PILED SNOW FOR WINDBREAK

SNOW WALL

VESTIBULE

←—TRENCH FOR EASY ENTRY

SKI-PACKED PLATFORM
FOR TENT

"DEADMAN"

BRANCH OR
LOG BURIED
IN THE SNOW

pitch the tent as tightly as possible. A tightly pitched tent is at its strongest. Stake the tent out snugly at all possible points. Stretch it tight via the reinforced points that allow taut lines. Setting stakes in winter requires a particular technique. The stakes need to be pushed deep, and the snow should be allowed to sinter around them. Even then, stakes might melt out over time, and the tent will lose its tautness. You can use skis, poles, and ice axes, if you don't need them for their intended purposes, as stakes to provide greater stability.

Snow also allows the possibility of staking out the tent with a few deadmen. If possible, use a stick one to two feet long as a deadman. Buried gear—like a stuff sack filled with snow—also works, but it can be hard to dig back out after a night or two of sintering. To set a deadman, tie it with at least a couple of feet of cord to a stake-out point on the tent. The cord should be looped around the deadman, with the knot—a taut-line hitch, ideally—far enough from the deadman that it will be above the snow when placed; this will allow for tightening later on. Stomp aggressively into the snow with your booted foot at the appropriate distance. Set the deadman in the bottom of the stomped hole and fill the hole with snow. Then stomp on the surface to help it set. You should place all of your deadmen and let them sinter before tightening any of them.

If a strong wind whips through camp before the tent is set, the procedure is more prob-

TIDYING UP

Falling or windblown snow may bury anything left lying around. Before hitting the sack, tidy up the camp. Some nights, tidying up won't make a major difference, but wise winter campers are storm-proof every night. Better to be safe than sorry. Pick up litter, and store all items in packs or in the kitchen. Stick your skis and poles upright in the snow (but don't let the baskets of your ski poles stick into the snow and get frozen, requiring digging and possible damage to remove them). Then tether lightweight sleds to the skis or poles. Move all your clothing into the tent or under the tarp, and store your pack in the shelter or secured to your sled. Also, fill the stoves and get things ready for morning so you can minimize chores for the following day.

lematic. Securely stake out the upwind side of the tent before placing any of the tent poles. If the tent has a fly, it is less likely to become a kite if someone holds on to it while someone else attaches it to the tent. Holding the fly down during a strong wind also helps minimize the tangle of knots in the lines attached to the fly.

TARPS

Whether you're using a simple or pyramid-shaped tarp, the differences between tarp camping and tent camping are minimal. First, stomp out a platform and let it work-harden. Hang and secure the tarp at a steep angle—you definitely want the snow to slide off rather than build up. Once the tarp is hung between trees, dig out the snow from underneath to give yourself more living space and protection from wind. If you bevel the sides of the space beneath the tarp, cutting into the snow away from the living space, you can add even more room. Pack the dug-out snow into the spaces around the edges of the tarp, especially if it has open ends, to enclose your living space. You'll end up with a nice room roofed with the tarp.

SNOW SHELTERS

There is fun, satisfaction, a touch of wonder, and a bit of magic involved in creating a home out of snow. If you haven't used one before, you will be surprised how peaceful and quiet it is inside—a howling wind becomes a muffled hush—and how the soft flicker of a candle creates a wonderland of light. You will also be surprised by how much warmer it is than a tent. When the temperature plunges to minus 40 degrees F, a good snow shelter will likely be 70 degrees warmer inside than outside. You can leave behind the weight of a tent or tarp, and you can construct a snow shelter to fit a group of just about any size (though novices should stick to shelters that hold two to four people). Furthermore, the ability to make a snow shelter may be life-saving in an emergency. On the downside, snow shelters are a lot of work—work that takes time and burns energy—and most winter campers who build snow shelters don't move

SETTING UP A TARP

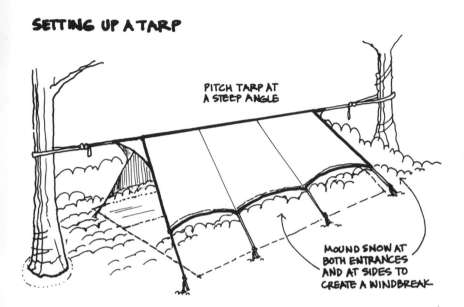

PITCH TARP AT A STEEP ANGLE

MOUND SNOW AT BOTH ENTRANCES AND AT SIDES TO CREATE A WINDBREAK

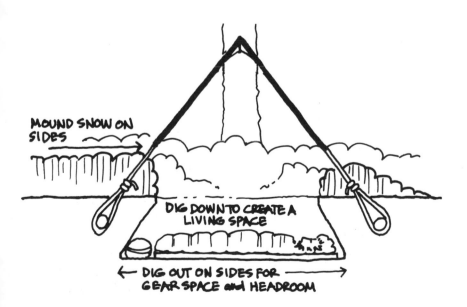

MOUND SNOW ON SIDES

DIG DOWN TO CREATE A LIVING SPACE

← DIG OUT ON SIDES FOR → GEAR SPACE and HEADROOM

SLEEPING AND WAKING UP WARM

In addition to sleeping in a safe spot, you need to sleep warm. The basic idea, says Shannon Rochelle, NOLS winter camping instructor, is to "enter your bag as warm and dry as you can be." Here are some tips:

- Eat a hearty dinner, with plenty of fat, and drink lots of fluids before retiring. You need the fuel and fluids to burn during the long, cold night.
- Warm yourself up before you bed down. Go for a walk, ski, shovel some snow, do sit-ups or push-ups. You don't want to enter your bag sweaty, but you do want to be toasty.
- Before crawling into the shelter, brush the snow off your clothing and boots (some people use a small whisk broom for this job). Don't take any unnecessary moisture into the shelter.
- Remove your clothing down to the layers you'll sleep in. The more layers you wear to bed, the better insulated you'll be. You are seeking a balance, however. Too much clothing compresses the dead air space, reducing your insulation. Too little clothing may let the chill in. And be sure to sleep in loose-fitting clothing: tight clothing reduces circulation.
- Replace any damp layers of clothing with dry layers. Take special care to sleep in dry socks. If your feet tend to get cold, wear down or synthetic booties, or shove your feet into a pile jacket or sweater.
- Sleep in a comfortable cap or a balaclava. The brain will sacrifice the rest of the body to save itself, so don't give it a reason.
- Place slightly damp clothing in your sleeping bag, near the trunk of your body, to dry overnight.
- Place extra dry layers of clothing inside your sleeping bag, if there's adequate room. They can also be shaped into a comfy pillow. Put outer layers that you aren't wearing between you and the ground for insulation. If the outer layers are relatively dry, put them between your sleeping bag and your top sleeping pad. If they're damp, put them between your sleeping pads.
- To prevent freezing, place leather boots and boot liners in your sleeping bag's stuff sack (turned inside out), and place the stuff sack between your legs.
- Put a full water bottle and a snack in your sleeping bag in case you need to fire up the internal furnace during the night. Or keep an insulated container of hot, sweet tea or chocolate in your tent. Be sure to distinguish the water bottle from the pee bottle.
- Sleep with your face out to prevent the moisture of respiration from building up in your bag. Wear a scarf around your neck or a neck gaiter rather than cinching up the drawcord of a mummy bag around your head.
- You'll probably wake up several times during the night, to urinate or just to change position. This is normal in cold weather. Don't waste energy trying to fight the urge to urinate. Moving around gets your circulation stirred up, generating a bit of heat.

every day. But if you decide to build one, all you need, in addition to time and energy, is a shovel and a lot of snow.

Although you might be able to build an adequate snow shelter based on the instructions in this chapter, the best way to learn is from an experienced constructor of snow shelters who can tailor the project to the unique terrain and, even more importantly, to local snow conditions. Taking shortcuts in these procedures may lead to a snow shelter collapse.

Site and Shelter Selection: General Guidelines

Any site for a snow shelter needs to have, in addition to snow, subfreezing temperatures. Avoid building a snow shelter when the temperature allows melting, because the snow will be too weak and too heavy. The conditions that make a site safe and comfortable for a snow shelter are generally the same as those described in the beginning of this chapter. Wind, however, is

---

MAINTAINING WARMTH IN THE MORNING

- Do a few sit-ups or stretches while still in your bag. This generates a little body heat before you expose yourself to the cold.
- Dress quickly to prevent loss of body heat. Put on your boots while they and your feet are still warm from the bag. It's much more efficient to maintain body heat than to generate it.
- Get the stove going, and stoke the internal furnace. There's nothing like a hot drink and a hot breakfast to ease the stress of the cold. Try to drink at least a quart of liquid. Consider cooking extra food and packing it for a quick lunch.
- Move your stuff outside. Hang clothing that still feels damp on tree limbs or ski poles. Hang your sleeping bag inside out between your skis stuck in the snow. The outside air is generally drier than the air inside the shelter, and the drier the air, the faster your things will dry out.
- If you have a tent, pull the stakes (unless the wind is whipping through camp) and turn the tent on its side to allow the bottom to dry before packing it. Don't pack or haul any more weight than you need to.
- Use teamwork to help speed up the morning chores: have some people cook while others pack.

BASIC PRINCIPLES OF SNOW SHELTER CONSTRUCTION

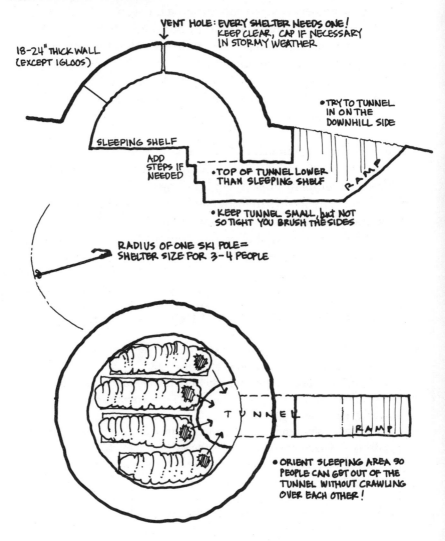

VENT HOLE: EVERY SHELTER NEEDS ONE! KEEP CLEAR, CAP IF NECESSARY IN STORMY WEATHER

18-24" THICK WALL (EXCEPT IGLOOS)

• TRY TO TUNNEL IN ON THE DOWNHILL SIDE

SLEEPING SHELF

ADD STEPS IF NEEDED

• TOP OF TUNNEL LOWER THAN SLEEPING SHELF

RAMP

• KEEP TUNNEL SMALL, but NOT SO TIGHT YOU BRUSH THE SIDES

RADIUS OF ONE SKI POLE = SHELTER SIZE FOR 3-4 PEOPLE

TUNNEL

RAMP

• ORIENT SLEEPING AREA SO PEOPLE CAN GET OUT OF THE TUNNEL WITHOUT CRAWLING OVER EACH OTHER!

not as big of a problem with a snow shelter, so a more open spot can be chosen. Specific conditions required for each type of snow shelter are discussed on the following pages.

Whatever type of shelter you choose, start small and simple. Smaller shelters take less work and, more importantly, tend to be stronger. With the same wall thickness, for instance, a small sphere is stronger than a large sphere, not only because the walls are fatter in relation to the space they enclose, but also because smaller spheres have sharper angles, which makes for stronger structures. The type of shelter you choose also depends on the type of snow:

> Drifted snow—snow cave or digloo
> Wind slab—igloo
> Deep, soft snow—quinzhee
> Shallow, soft snow—quinzhee
> Wet snow—tent or tarp

Snow Caves
In places around the world where the snow lingers long, humans have developed different types of snow shelters. The earliest, the easiest, and the most common is probably the snow cave—a tunnel to a room dug into an existing snowdrift. The construction of a snow cave be divided into four steps: site selection, tunnel construction, room construction, and finishing touches.

Site Selection
Even when the snowpack lies relatively thin, you may be able to find suitable drifts. Look downwind of large open spaces, where the wind naturally slows down and deposits snow. Look for drifts on the leeward side of ridges, along stream banks, in the lee of the first trees downwind of a meadow or lake, or in gullies downwind of open areas. Ideally, the site should have a five- to ten-degree slope to help trap heat in the cave. At a minimum, you'll need six feet of snow, but ten feet or more is better.

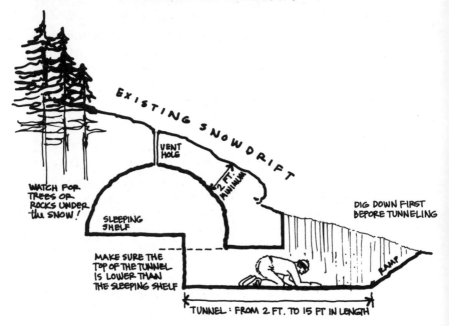

SNOW CAVE: A TUNNEL TO A ROOM DUG INTO AN EXISTING SNOWDRIFT

EXISTING SNOWDRIFT

VENT HOLE

2 FT. MINIMUM

DIG DOWN FIRST BEFORE TUNNELING

WATCH FOR TREES OR ROCKS UNDER the SNOW!

SLEEPING SHELF

RAMP

MAKE SURE THE TOP OF THE TUNNEL IS LOWER THAN THE SLEEPING SHELF

TUNNEL: FROM 2 FT. TO 15 FT IN LENGTH

STEP 1 : SITE SELECTION : PROBE! FOR POSSIBLE OBSTRUCTIONS.

STEP 2 : CONSTRUCT THE TUNNEL. YOU MAY NEED TO DIG A TRENCH FIRST IF THE SNOW IS DEEP.

STEP 3 : DIG UP TO CONSTRUCT ROOM.

STEP 4 : ADD FINISHING TOUCHES: VENTILATION HOLE, SLEEPING PLATFORM, ETC.

To check the depth of the snow with accuracy, you'll need something to probe with. In the absence of an actual probe, you can use ski poles that screw together. You can also probe with an adjustable-length ski pole, but be warned that it may come apart, leaving you digging for the other half. Remember, you need to probe the depth of the snow not only top to bottom but also horizontally. A thorough job of probing can help you avoid having rocks or large "house plants" in your shelter. Feel free to add some snow to the top to make it deeper.

You can stick some poles about two feet in for the diggers to use as gauges. Once digging commences, stay off your new roof.

Tunnel Construction

There are infinite variations in the building of a snow cave, but the basic construction remains the same. It is generally best to start digging from the downhill side, below the drift. Dig down into the snow. In deep snow, you'll be digging a trench that is about as deep as you are tall. In shallower snow, you'll dig to the ground. Digging down into the snow first gives you more snow to dig up into for the room. You can toss the snow you're removing onto what will be the roof of the cave for even more depth.

> **NOLS TIP**
>
> **Dress for Digging**
>
> *As a digger, you're going to get wet, so dress accordingly. Prepare by losing a layer or two of clothing to reduce sweating, but wear a waterproof—or at least water-resistant—shell to stay as dry as possible from melting snow. Some people dig tunnels and caves with a closed-cell foam sleeping pad under them to stay a bit drier—and warmer.*

Then dig a tunnel into the drift. This will be the entryway, or porch. Tunnel height depends largely on drift depth. Taller tunnels are easier to dig, even though there's more snow to move, because you aren't slithering around like a fleece-scaled reptile. A critical factor, however, is this: the top of the tunnel entrance must be lower than the base of the sleeping chamber, in order to trap heat. The tunnel should also be wide enough so your elbows don't brush the sides. It should be rounded at the top to prevent sagging and help you to avoid brushing the top of it with your head. It can be as short as two feet or as long as five feet. A longer tunnel gives you the option of an indoor kitchen (see page 159). A shorter tunnel, of course, is much easier to dig and to get in and out of.

Room Construction

When the tunnel is long enough, dig up to remove the snow for the sleeping chamber. The size of the room will depend, once again, on the size of the drift, but also on the number of people intending to sleep there. Moving the snow typically becomes a much bigger problem at this point. Keep pushing the loose snow toward the tunnel's mouth with your feet, where it will be shoveled out later.

The minimum thickness of the walls and ceiling should be about a foot, with two feet being better. Thicker walls are more stable and insulate better. You should probe, now and then, to check thickness. If you see light coming through, you may be getting a little too thin. Back off and dig gently. You may need to have someone block the light coming into the tunnel so that you can see thin spots more easily. If you used poles as gauges when selecting your site, you'll have an easier time determining thickness. Cut the snow—don't pry or chop (this can't be overemphasized), or you might bust a hole through to the surface, which is virtually impossible to fix. The interior should be dome-shaped and relatively smooth, with at least enough room for you to sit up comfortably. The dome shape is strong, and smoothness prevents water from dripping as the cave warms up. Although most of the shaping will be done with a shovel, a gloved hand works well for the final smoothing.

Snow caves seldom collapse after the temperature has dropped at night and the overall strength of the walls and roof has increased. An exception might be if someone accidentally walks across the roof. Using some type of marker, such as snow blocks or upright skis, to indicate the presence of the snow cave is not a bad idea. Occasionally during construction, a cave fails, especially when a digger has been prying with a shovel instead of cutting. To be safe, keep at least one person outside during construction to dig out anyone who gets buried, and have your diggers wear avalanche transceivers.

> **N O L S   T I P**
>
> **Watch for Blue Light**
>
> *When you can see blue light coming through a snow wall, you can estimate that the wall is twelve to eighteen inches thick.*

Finishing Touches

Now you can add a few finishing touches to make your snow cave more safe and satisfying. A ventilation hole in the top of the room is mandatory. Without ventilation, room air grows stale, and the humidity can rise to the point where everything inside gets damp. Adequate ventilation also helps prevent sagging in the snowy roof due to overheating. The warmer the outside temperature, the bigger the vent hole needs to be. At an ambient air temperature of 30 degrees F, the vent should be about four inches wide; at 0 degrees F, it should be about two inches; and at minus 30 degrees F, a one-inch-wide vent is sufficient. You can poke through the roof with a ski pole or stick to make the vent. Don't worry about snow falling down the vent: humid air will rise out of it all night with enough velocity to carry snowflakes up and out. You can build a chimney—a long block with a well-placed hole—if you expect high winds and drifting that might plug the vent. In all cases, check the vent hole often to make sure it stays open.

Digloos

A digloo is a snow cave that can be dug from the top and the side at the same time. The final result is the same: a dome-shaped room accessible via a tunnel. A digloo requires the same depth of snow as a snow cave—a minimum of five to six feet, with ten feet or more being better. The disadvantage of a digloo is the need for snow blocks to cap the hole in the roof. The process of making and setting snow blocks is more complex than the simple digging of a snow cave. The primary advantages of a digloo over a snow cave are that two people can dig at the same time, so the work tends to go faster, and snow doesn't have to be burrowed into and ferried down a tunnel.

After probing to find an appropriate depth, ski-pack the snow above the building site. An area about six feet square is sufficient for two people. The sleeping chamber will be located below this work-hardened area, and the packed snow provides a foundation for the cap blocks. If the snowpack is

DIGLOO: A DOME-SHAPED ROOM ACCESSIBLE BY TUNNEL.

BASICALLY, A SNOW CAVE THAT CAN BE DUG FROM THE
TOP AND THE SIDE AT THE SAME TIME.

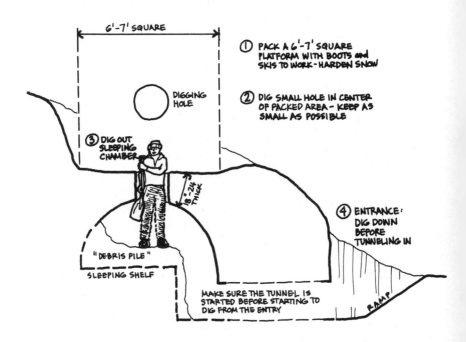

6'-7' SQUARE

DIGGING HOLE

① PACK A 6'-7' SQUARE PLATFORM WITH BOOTS and SKIS TO WORK-HARDEN SNOW

② DIG SMALL HOLE IN CENTER OF PACKED AREA - KEEP AS SMALL AS POSSIBLE

③ DIG OUT SLEEPING CHAMBER

18"-24" THICK

④ ENTRANCE: DIG DOWN BEFORE TUNNELING IN

"DEBRIS PILE"

SLEEPING SHELF

MAKE SURE THE TUNNEL IS STARTED BEFORE STARTING TO DIG FROM THE ENTRY

RAMP

⑤ CUT BLOCKS FROM PLATFORM and CAP THE DIGLOO

FIRST TWO BLOCKS

DIGGING HOLE IN TOP OF DIGLOO

ADD A THIRD BLOCK

CAP BLOCK

SHOVEL ON LOOSE SNOW TO FILL IN HOLES BETWEEN BLOCKS

relatively shallow, shovel some extra snow on top of the packed platform to raise it. The shoveled snow doesn't need to be boot-packed, but it should be tamped with a shovel to firm it. This initial packing is best done as soon as you've chosen a site. Other parts of construction must wait, since you need to allow time for the packed snow to sinter, making it possible to dig a stable hole.

Unless you're very far north or south, in the Arctic or Antarctic, you'll probably need to make a quarry from which to cut blocks. Boot-packing an area about eight feet square will provide ample blocks for a digloo. Just smash the snow up with your boots for a while, and then ski-pack the top smooth. It is easier to cut good blocks out of a quarry with a smooth top. Don't walk on the quarry after it has been smoothed, or you will crack the snow. This is another job that should be done early, so it can strengthen by sintering. For instance, if you break trail to a snow shelter site the day before you move camp to that site, you can make a quarry that will yield industrial-strength blocks.

Once it has firmed up—a process that takes at least an hour or two—dig a round hole in the center of the packed area above the future digloo. Make the hole just big enough to sneak the shovel in and out of with the digger standing in it. The smaller the hole, the easier it will be to cap with blocks. Carefully avoid stepping on the hard snow immediately around the hole. If you do plunge into the snow, fill the accidental hole with packed snow, and try not to set a block corner on that weak spot later. (If the snow is too dry to pack into your mistake, you can make a quick-setting "epoxy" with water and snow.) Dig down a couple of feet, and then start digging to the sides, carving an inverted funnel shape in the snow. This will be the sleeping chamber. As the chamber grows, it will become easier to stand in the hole while you dig. Dig to the ground as you widen the bottom of the hole or, in deeper snow, until you have a room the size you want. Basic snow shelter construction principles are important here—the dome shape of the room, the smooth ceiling, and cutting the snow rather than prying out large chunks.

As you pitch snow from the hole, try to create a rough snow wall to remind others to stay off the roof of the digloo. Shape a floor that slopes very slightly toward the intended door. Leave some "debris" inside—snow you've dug out for the room—to fill holes that tend to show up in the floor and for finishing touches. When the room is relatively complete, begin to dig toward the tunnel, and the second digger.

The second digger begins about ten feet downhill from the packed area, digging straight down, following the directions for a snow cave. The goal here is a clean face on the uphill side. Then a tunnel is dug uphill, toward where the room is being constructed. The tunnel digger may move faster than the room digger, and a lot of unnecessary energy can be wasted digging the tunnel too far. Estimate the length needed for the tunnel, dig it out, and back off until the room is complete.

When the digger in the room starts to dig toward the tunnel, the tunnel digger can resume digging until both ends of the tunnel are joined. From this point on, the snow can be removed via the tunnel.

On a steep slope, leave enough of the snowpack on the bottom of the tunnel to build large steps. Steps are difficult, if not impossible, to add later.

With the tunnel and room complete, it's time to cut blocks from the quarry. Blocks can be cut with a snow saw, a wood saw, or, if you're careful and skillful, a wide shovel. A good block size is about eighteen to twenty inches wide, two feet long, and six inches thick. Square the blocks as much as possible, leaving the corners intact. The work goes faster with bigger blocks, but smaller blocks are easier to handle. If the blocks are too heavy, consider making them thinner rather than narrower and shorter. If one long side of a block is obviously fatter, and thus heavier, than the other side, place the heavier side down for better balance.

Carry the blocks to the edge of the roof of the digloo, and pass them to someone standing inside the hole. Lean the blocks against each other at about a forty-five-degree angle, with their "feet" on top of the packed circle at the edge of the opening. Each block should rest on its corners, not the middle, or it will rock and be unstable. A bit of mitering may help, but don't try to shape the blocks too much—this often leaves you needing more blocks. The force of the blocks leaning against each other increases their strength over time. If the hole is no more than three feet across, three blocks should be enough. A smaller, lighter block is needed to cap the pyramid. Ideally, this final cap block should fit snugly, with no rocking. You can accomplish this best by setting the cap in place and sawing gently from the inside, mitering the block until it fits snugly. Chink the large holes left in the triangle of blocks by shoveling softer snow from the outside until the cap is sealed. Now you can vent the room and add finishing touches, such as storage shelves and sleeping platforms, as desired.

Igloos

Igloos are domed shelters built out of snow blocks. They are the most complex type of snow shelters and the most demanding of your time and energy. And an igloo can't be built unless you can find or create some really hard snow. Igloos are generally built in coastal regions because of the abundance of wind-hammered slabs of snow that is too hard to dig into. Wind and warm temperatures naturally compress the snow, so strong blocks can be cut directly from the snow-pack. When firm snow isn't available, a digloo-style quarry must be prepared that is about four times the size of the base of the igloo.

Begin by ski-packing a foundation for the igloo. If you can build your igloo on a slope of five to ten degrees, it will help you make a downslope door that traps heat. Within the ski-packed area, draw an exact circle in the snow that marks the outside of your intended sleeping area. You can improvise a compass out of ski poles to mark the circle: Stick one ski pole in the snow in the center of the area. Put the strap of the other pole over the pole in the snow, and move it down to snow level. Now you can draw a circle in the snow with a radius of approximately the length of your ski pole. With most poles,

IGLOO: DOMED SHELTER BUILT OUT OF SNOW BLOCKS

USEFUL IN AREAS WITH WINDHAMMERED SNOW, WHICH IS STRONG BUT ALSO HARD TO DIG OUT.

* A QUARRY FOR CUTTING SNOW BLOCKS NEEDS TO BE AT LEAST 4 TIMES THE SIZE OF THE BASE OF THE IGLOO.

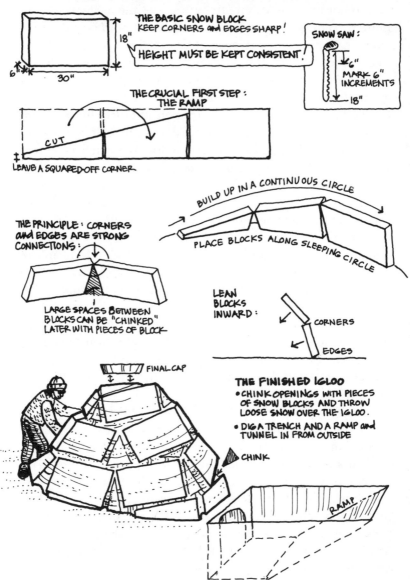

THE BASIC SNOW BLOCK
KEEP CORNERS and EDGES SHARP!

18"

HEIGHT MUST BE KEPT CONSISTENT!

6"   30"

SNOW SAW:
6"
MARK 6" INCREMENTS
18"

THE CRUCIAL FIRST STEP:
THE RAMP

CUT

LEAVE A SQUARED-OFF CORNER

BUILD UP IN A CONTINUOUS CIRCLE

PLACE BLOCKS ALONG SLEEPING CIRCLE

THE PRINCIPLE: CORNERS and EDGES ARE STRONG CONNECTIONS:

LARGE SPACES BETWEEN BLOCKS CAN BE "CHINKED" LATER WITH PIECES OF BLOCK

LEAN BLOCKS INWARD:
CORNERS
EDGES

FINAL CAP

THE FINISHED IGLOO
• CHINK OPENINGS WITH PIECES OF SNOW BLOCKS AND THROW LOOSE SNOW OVER THE IGLOO.
• DIG A TRENCH AND A RAMP and TUNNEL IN FROM OUTSIDE

CHINK

RAMP

you'll end up with an igloo than can house three or four people. Keep in mind that the snow blocks will take up some of the room inside the circle, so plan accordingly.

Walk around the circle in your boots, being sure to press hard enough to bust through the snow layers, compressing the snow into strong supports to hold up the walls. Now shovel some fresh snow onto the packed area, smooth it out, and let it set up while you cut blocks.

There is more than one way to build an igloo. The method described here is for a rectangular block type, which offers the greatest hope of success for a novice builder. Rectangular blocks make stronger domes than angled (mitered) blocks do. These relatively easy-to-build igloos are not only strong but also functional, having withstood the extreme winds and temperatures of Arctic winters.

Using a snow saw, cut rectangular blocks that are as large as you can handle—six by eighteen by thirty inches is a good size. These blocks can be shaped into a beautiful spiral by laying them on their long side. It is essential that they be a uniform height (about eighteen inches is suggested). You'll need a standard to measure by, and the length of the blade of your snow saw will work fine.

The igloo will be held up by the corners of the blocks. Move the blocks with care, taking pains not to break off any corners during handling. Avoid using blocks that have crumbly snow in the corners. If the blocks are heavier on one side, they will balance better if the heavier side is placed down.

After you've cut out the first block, you'll need to shape it to form a ramp that initiates a spiral. By spiraling the blocks, you will have them leaning even more into each other, and thus bonding more quickly and firmly. Cut from the middle of one end to a far corner so that you have two slanted blocks, one about one and a half to two times larger than the other. Don't cut to the exact corner, or it will chip off—leave that thin corner about one to two inches thick for strength. When you flip over the cut piece and set it in place, the spiraling wall has begun.

If your igloo is on a slope, set the ramp so that it starts near the highest point of the circle and slopes down—a method that holds the ramp at an angle, making the next course of blocks easier to deal with and the overall result prettier. The ramp needs to have the outside of the block exactly on the circle, so it is supported by work-hardened snow. If the walls are not built on stable snow, you'll get substantial sagging overnight. Set the first whole block next to the high end of the ramp and with a slight but obvious lean. If it's made of very strong snow, you may want to cut the inside of the top corner off to leave a little bevel, where it will rest against the preceding block. Place it on the circle, and slide it home against the first block. Hold it for about five seconds. Release it to see if it stays firmly in place. If it doesn't, pull it back and slide it in again until it does stay. If the block rocks left and right, flip it up and cut out some of the middle of the bottom, giving it feet to rest on.

Keep setting blocks with an obvious lean until you've gone all the way around the circle. Don't worry about the large open triangles between blocks; they indicate that the blocks are leaning well against each other and the igloo is structurally sound. Each higher course of blocks needs to lean more than the preceding one—a critical aspect of any dome. This first course of blocks should be the heaviest blocks.

Start the next course of blocks on top of the ramp, being careful not to place the corners of the new blocks directly above the corners of the blocks of the first course. Otherwise, you will have less stability and a less smooth interior surface. Remember that this entire course needs a more distinctive lean than the first course. Your intent isn't to build walls but a roof. More lean means fewer blocks for the same size igloo.

The third course will take fewer blocks, depending on the size of the igloo. The third course needs a radical lean of forty-five degrees. Be bold about leaning; it's better to lean too far and break a block or two than it is to build a towering structure using far too many blocks.

Keep spiraling inward, using blocks lighter in weight, until you can set a horizontal block to cap the igloo. Trim the final blocks with a snow saw to maximize a good fit. Leave an adequate vent hole in the top of the igloo, the same as you would for a snow cave or digloo.

Now you can chink the holes, but there's no hurry. Some people prefer to wait an hour or two, allowing the blocks to freeze together more firmly before chinking. When you are ready to chink, cut triangles of snow a little bigger than the openings, and taper them into a wedge shape that lets you press the chinks into the holes. Gravity will settle these chinks into a structurally sound position. After chinking, gently shovel a little soft snow onto the dome to provide extra insulation and protection from the wind and sun.

Dig a door by tunneling straight down from inside the igloo—the block-setter is sealed off inside—at the edge of the floor. Keep the tunnel just barely big enough to crawl through. You can enlarge it later, if you wish, after the structure has firmed up, but remember that doorway has to support the wall above it. Have someone outside begin a horizontal tunnel that will end up meeting the tunnel from inside. A longer tunnel generally helps keep the igloo warmer. The most important aspect of the door is the heat-trapping effect. If the highest part of the tunnel ceiling is lower than the floor you sleep on, you will trap heat well enough.

Quinzhees

Many areas do not commonly have adequate snow depth or appropriate snow type to build caves or igloos. In these circumstances, you can build a quinzhee, which is a hollowed-out pile of snow—a pile that you make. This type of snow shelter was traditionally used by the Athabascans on the taiga and is appropriate in the dry snows of the Rockies. You can build a quinzhee with less than two feet of snow on the ground.

Follow the directions given earlier to choose a site for the pile of snow. Determine the quinzhee's size by drawing a rough circle big enough to house all the intended occupants without touching the walls. For a group of four, you can create a workable circle by rotating a 170 cm ski around a pole placed upright in the center. A large group may choose to build several smaller quinzhees, since smaller snow structures generally have stronger walls. Walk around the rim of the circle to break up the soft snow so that it will harden. This is important, because the walls will be two to three feet thick at the base, and you'll need firm footing for these walls. Be sure that some of your steps punch all the way to the ground. Not doing this can lead to collapse of the structure while hollowing it out. Be careful not to pack the middle of the circle. That's the part you're going to dig out, so you want to leave the snow there as easy to move as possible. You can even throw tightly closed packs and well-protected sleeping bags in the middle as filler, before you start shoveling. If you have a long, slim pole, place it upright in the middle of the area to serve as a guide, telling the digger when the middle of the pile has been reached.

When you start shoveling snow into a pile—the not-so-fun part of construction—throw softer snow where the wall will be, since it will sinter into a stronger uniform density. Toss any chunks of snow into the middle. Chunks have air spaces around them, making them easy to dig out, and using chunks in the wall would leave holes. You can also throw crumbling snow into the middle. It, too, will be easy to dig out later. Keep piling up snow until the mound is large and dome shaped. It should have no points or horizontal flat spots on it, characteristics that create weakness in the walls.

When the pile is large enough, pack the snow on the outside with a ski or the flat of a shovel. This increases the density of the outer wall, and it also shortens the time for sintering to occur. The pile of snow must firm up substantially before you can hollow it out. Sintering happens slowly when the snowpack is cold and quickly when the snow is warm. You can speed up the sintering process by double-packing the walls and roof: pack, add snow, and pack it again. In bitterly cold conditions, it's best to wait a couple of hours before hollowing. When it's warm, you can dig almost immediately,

QUINZHEE: A PILE OF SNOW YOU MAKE and THEN HOLLOW OUT INTO A SHELTER

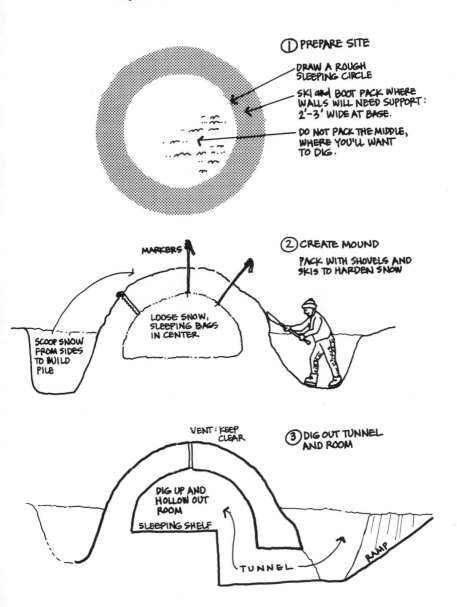

① PREPARE SITE

DRAW A ROUGH SLEEPING CIRCLE

SKI and BOOT PACK WHERE WALLS WILL NEED SUPPORT: 2'-3' WIDE AT BASE.

DO NOT PACK THE MIDDLE, WHERE YOU'LL WANT TO DIG.

② CREATE MOUND

PACK WITH SHOVELS AND SKIS TO HARDEN SNOW

MARKERS

LOOSE SNOW, SLEEPING BAGS IN CENTER

SCOOP SNOW FROM SIDES TO BUILD PILE

③ DIG OUT TUNNEL AND ROOM

VENT: KEEP CLEAR

DIG UP AND HOLLOW OUT ROOM

SLEEPING SHELF

TUNNEL

RAMP

although too much rushing increases the risk of collapse. If the snowpack is so warm that it feels wet, don't build a quinzhee.

After the pile of snow has firmed up adequately, start to tunnel in from the lowest side of the mound. But first, discuss rescue procedures in case the snow collapses on the "mole" digging out the inside. Keep the tunnel as low and as small as possible. You can easily enlarge an entrance, but you can rarely make one smaller. As soon as you're in a couple of feet, start hollowing out the quinzhee. Once you can kneel and then stand, you'll get less wet while digging. Many people like to work quickly to the center of the room for a better frame of reference for digging. Be careful to cut the snow and not pry it with the shovel—prying puts unnecessary stress on the still-sintering walls.

From the middle of the mound, dig up, keeping the interior in a dome shape (no flat spots or points). Leave a layer of snow for the floor. And once again, for the most efficient heat-trapping, make the floor higher than the top of the door.

Hollow out the room until you can see a little blue light showing through the snow. If there's too much bright light coming in the door, have someone block the entrance. Once you see light in an area of the ceiling, dig elsewhere. Once you see light all over the interior of the dome, smooth out the ceiling. Instead of using light to estimate wall thickness, you can use markers, such as ski poles, stuck into the mound before the hollowing-out process. Stick them in about two feet, the approximate wall thickness you want. When you reach the markers from the inside, you can stop digging. Pack the floor by crawling around on it, and then smooth it out as flat as possible. Put a vent in the roof to draw off moisture (as for snow caves), and leave for a while to allow the floor to sinter.

During the hollowing-out process, the snow pile may occasionally settle with a disturbing "whoomp." The lighter and colder the snow, the more likely this is to happen. Don't worry—this seldom signals a collapse. However, you may want to dig a bit less aggressively or stop and double-pack the walls before continuing to hollow out the interior.

The larger the quinzhee, the trickier the construction. Larger quinzhees require thicker walls. If you want to house an especially large group, make the snow pile longer instead of wider, sort of a Quonset hut shape. This ovate shape gives full strength to conventional snow walls but allows for virtually infinite expansion lengthwise. With a really long quinzhee, you can tunnel in from both ends and seal one entrance later.

MAINTAINING YOUR SNOW SHELTER

- Keep the vent clear to preserve air flow.
- Do not burn stoves and lanterns that consume oxygen unless they have special hooded ventilation systems.
- Lay out ground cloths and sleeping pads so they overlap and cover cold spots.
- Keep warm items like sleeping bags away from the snow walls.
- Burn a candle for light and a pleasant atmosphere.
- Watch for sagging or other shelter damage, and repair as necessary.

Repairing Snow Shelters

As in most situations, prevention is easier than reparation when it comes to snow shelters. To avoid damage, plan and route pathways well away from snow shelters. Build little walls of snow or set up markers to remind campers which areas to avoid. In the dark of night, half asleep and full of urine, it's not that difficult to forget where the roof of the snow shelter is. Build your shelter appropriately, and ventilate it adequately.

Even well-built snow shelters, however, drop an inch or two every day due to natural settling of the snowpack. A big storm or unusually warm temperatures can greatly increase the rate of sagging, but the main culprit is usually your own body heat in a poorly vented shelter. This problem can often be managed by reshaping the living space from within. But first, add more snow to the outside and let it sinter; then shave off more

BUILDING A SUPPORT PILLAR
FOR A SAGGING SNOW SHELTER

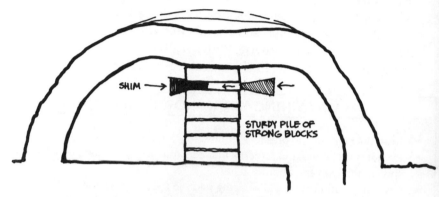

SHIM →

STURDY PILE OF
STRONG BLOCKS

1. BUILD A STURDY PILE OF STRONG BLOCKS.
2. PRESS THE TOP BLOCK AGAINST THE ROOF/
   CEILING OF THE SAGGING SNOW SHELTER.
3. DRIVE PIECES OF SNOW BLOCK — "SHIMS" —
   BETWEEN THE TOP BLOCK and THE STACK
   FOR A TIGHT FIT. MEASURE SAG WITH A
   SKI POLE OR OTHER OBJECT.
4. BE PREPARED TO BUILD ANOTHER SNOW SHELTER!

of the inside. This is easy to do if you deal with it early in the
sagging process.

If sagging is extreme, it's possible to use snow blocks as
pillars to support a seriously sagging ceiling section. A pillar
will consume a lot of floor space, but it's preferable to building a new shelter. To build a pillar with blocks, make sure that
the blocks are dense, uniform, and strong. The pillar stands
from the floor to the sag in the ceiling, and the final block
needs to be shimmed for a tight fit. (Shims are wedges of
snow driven between blocks.) When driven between the top
block and the one below it, shims firmly and evenly press the
top block against the ceiling. Shim from all sides to keep from
canting the top block. Once you start packing the shims in

tight, work quickly, because the high
pressure will cause rapid sintering.

Small holes in roofs and walls are
easy to patch. Cut a chunk of dense
snow—anything you can pick up
without it crumbling—and set it on
the hole. Seal it in place with soft
snow. If no snow is dense enough,
make a small quarry in order to build
a suitable block. You can also consider
making small repairs with the
makeshift "epoxy" mentioned on
page 147.

Big holes are much more of a challenge. You can throw a
tarp over the hole, weight it down with a little snow, and call
it good enough. It's also possible to fill large holes with snow
blocks, but you need high quality blocks, and the shelter
might not support the weight of the blocks. If the snow shelter
won't support the blocks, you'll have to build a pillar inside to
support them. In any case, repairing holes with blocks is a
time-consuming job requiring patience and finesse, and you
may decide to just start over.

Indoor Snow Kitchens

With deep enough snow and a large enough snow shelter, you
can build an indoor kitchen. However, it needs to be well-venti-
lated to get rid of the dangerous fumes and high humidity
caused by cooking, which means placing it near the entrance
with its own vent hole. (If you can't build an indoor kitchen
with good ventilation, you shouldn't build one at all.) The
advantages of an indoor kitchen include being able to fix breakfast without getting fully dressed and being able to prepare
meals while relatively warm and sheltered from storms. A
kitchen you can stand in is ideal, but you can sit or even kneel if
necessary.

To begin, sculpt a small counter in the shape of a half
dome—if the snow wall is thick enough. The half dome

should be high enough to accept the stove with your biggest pot set on it. Pack the flat surface gently with a shovel, and let it sinter for a while before stressing it. Then dig a vent straight up to the outside from where the stove will sit. The straighter the vent, the less melting will occur from the heat of the stove. The vent hole should be at least three inches wide.

From the outside, build a chimney for the vent, to encourage an updraft from the stove. The chimney can be constructed simply from four blocks of snow. If winds are gusting, you may need a chimney cap, a fifth block laid over the four already in place. If you use a cap, make sure that two of the blocks are shortened to allow the drafting of air underneath the cap. When you light the stove, expect the

INDOOR SNOW KITCHEN
ALCOVE FOR COOKING, WITH HOOD AND VENT

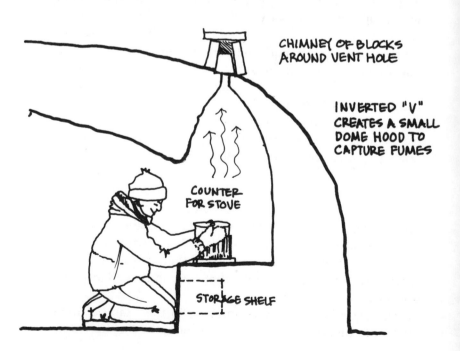

CHIMNEY OF BLOCKS AROUND VENT HOLE

INVERTED "V" CREATES A SMALL DOME HOOD TO CAPTURE FUMES

COUNTER FOR STOVE

STORAGE SHELF

first flames to gather momentum slowly as they heat up the chimney. Your indoor kitchen will circulate air whether in use or not. If you don't want the extra ventilation that brings in cool, dry air, stuff something into the kitchen's vent hole during periods of nonuse.

If snow falls at night, it could clog the chimney. A clogged chimney will not vent fumes, causing a noxious cloud to fill the interior of the shelter. Always be sure that the vent hole is open and air is flowing before firing up the stove.

Outdoor Snow Kitchens

In most cases, it's safer and easier to build an outdoor kitchen. By shoveling snow into a pile and digging down into it, you can carve out cooking platforms, tables, storage shelves, and even benches to sit on. You're limited only by your imagination—or lack of a shovel.

Choose a site for the kitchen that is out of the wind and that gets sun when you want it. Morning sun is especially appealing, so east-facing kitchens are generally preferable. If you've built a snow shelter, you may be able to situate the kitchen using the shelter as a windbreak and using part of the platform you've already work-hardened as part of the kitchen. Sites under overhanging conifers offer additional warmth at night, but beware of trees heavily laden with snow that could plop into your macaroni and cheese.

The snow for the kitchen needs to be work-hardened. You can do this by packing it with shovels or ski-packing. Without sintering, snow tends to crumble when you try to shape it and collapse when you walk on it.

After hardening, begin by shoveling snow out of the area that will be the floor, piling it up behind where the benches and counter will be. This snow offers wind protection and provides backs for seats, so pile it high rather than spreading it out. Make the floor wide enough so that people can sit on a bench on one side while others, such as those doing the cooking and snow melting, can move about freely on the other side.

OUTDOOR KITCHEN

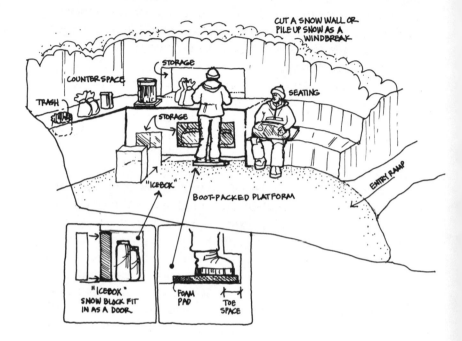

Benches should be wide enough to accept a sleeping pad as insulation. Consider making the bench seats high enough to keep your feet off the snow. This not only eliminates the conduction of heat from your feet to the snow but also takes pressure off your soles, allowing better circulation. The backs of the benches should be as high as possible and should lean back comfortably. If you've got the time, scoop out the seats of the bench for increased comfort.

Cooking counters should be at a comfortable height for working, high enough to avoid the need to lean over while preparing food. If you cut the counter into a high pile of snow, you'll have the additional benefit of a windbreak. Cut little storage areas into the snow behind and below the counter. Create spots for food bags, utensils, fuel, and spices. Below the counter, you can also cut out a hole in the banked snow to serve as a refrigerator. With a thick block of snow placed over the opening, the food you don't want frozen and the water you've made will stay thawed. All counters need toe spaces carved out under them, where the snow wall and floor meet, so you can stand against the counter with your legs touching it for easier reaching. As your creativity soars, you'll think of other refinements, such as a hole in the snow lined with a garbage bag for trash.

The stove needs a platform and a windscreen. If you don't have a windscreen, you can improvise one out of snow shovels, food bags, or snow walls built into the snow kitchen. (Snow walls, however, block the wind from only three sides.) With experimentation, you can sharpen your snow kitchen construction to a fine edge.

Emergency Snow Shelters

In an emergency, a life-saving snow shelter can be constructed quickly. You can dig a small snow cave in a drift—one just large enough for you to fit inside. Forget an actual tunnel, but if you can dig up slightly before scooping out the room, you'll trap more body heat. If you lack a shovel, improvise—dig with a pot, a ski, a signal mirror, even your gloved hands. Place your pack in front of the entrance hole as a door. A candle will brighten the interior and add degrees of warmth. Don't forget the vent hole. Without a sleeping pad, you can lie on extra clothing and, if you're in a forest, evergreen boughs.

If you're in the open or can't find a drift, dig a trench in the snow about three feet deep. Pile the snow from the trench on the windward side as a break. You can roof it with snow blocks (if you have the time to make them), evergreen boughs, or a tarp. Cover the roof with snow to add insulation.

An emergency shelter can sometimes be found. A hollow space under a downed tree is acceptable as long as the tree is naturally held firmly in place. Or, the space underneath a large, dense evergreen will provide some protection from the elements.

If you think people will be out searching for you, make your bivouac as visible as possible from the ground and the air by placing bright-colored clothing nearby or stomping an unusual pattern—such as "HELP"—in the snow. You can also sprinkle colorful drink powders such as Tang on the snow to attract attention. Remember that when you are inside the shelter, your ability to hear what is happening outside will be reduced to almost nothing. The temperature may drop and a storm may rage, but if you construct a simple shelter and carry basic emergency gear, you can be safe and secure in your shelter in the snow.

Appendix A

Leave No Trace

The wild lands of the world are, in many areas, being loved to death. Even though you may not see the impact of your visit, other than ski trails or compacted snow at campsites, lack of proper care for the environment will show up when the snow melts in spring. Through the combined efforts of the Leave No Trace Center for Outdoor Ethics and NOLS, and with the support of land management agencies, the national Leave No Trace educational program has helped reduce visitors' impact on the wilderness. The best time to start thinking about and making a commitment to Leave No Trace is early on, before you head out on an expedition. We are all responsible for the welfare of the outdoors.

The principles of Leave No Trace are guidelines, not rules. They are thoughtfully designed and based on scientific research, and they are intended to encourage you to act responsibly as stewards of the land, snow-covered or not. Learn all you can about the Leave No Trace program, understand what the seven principles mean, and keep them in mind at all times. It is not the intention of this book to thoroughly explore Leave No Trace but merely to point out some decisions you can make to minimize the impact of your visit. A more complete exploration of LNT's principles and tech-

niques can be found in *NOLS Soft Paths,* third edition, by
Bruce Hampton and David Cole.

PLAN AHEAD AND PREPARE

You should plan ahead with Leave No Trace in mind and prepare by learning how to implement the program's principles.
Take trash as an example. You could plan by repackaging
food, reducing the amount of garbage you will carry. Preparation would take the form of studying the best techniques for
packing out waste. One essential planning task is researching
local regulations, which should always win out over any of
the general guidelines in this book.

TRAVEL AND CAMP ON DURABLE SURFACES

Snow is a durable surface, so travel and camp on it as much as
possible. Most small mammals are active all winter, carrying on
the activities of life safely insulated beneath a blanket of snow.
Their subnivean environment (the environment beneath the
snow) is hard to hurt, except in two ways. First of all, skiers
compact the snow with their tracks, making dense lines that can
be difficult for small animals to climb over or burrow past. This
is hard to avoid but should be taken into account in soft, shallow
snowpacks. Secondly, removing snow down to the ground
removes the blanket of insulation and may allow the ground to
freeze, to the detriment of subnivean and subterranean life. Be
sure to cover the ground with snow again when you leave.

DISPOSE OF WASTE PROPERLY

The familiar expression is worth repeating: Pack it in, pack it
out. Always inspect your campsites and your rest-break spots,
and leave no waste behind. Carry garbage bags and pack out
leftover food as well as your trash, and lend a hand by packing
out the refuse discarded by others. In most cases, litter covered
by snow will be litter on the surface in a few months or less.

Avoid the thought that it doesn't matter where you defecate in snow. Use trailhead and backcountry toilets whenever
they are available. When they're not, defecate at least 200 feet

(about 70 adult paces) from any water source and well away from trails and campsites. Whenever possible, defecate at the base of a tree. Dig into the snow close to the trunk of the tree, down to the ground, or into the ground, if you can. Even if you can't, feces near a tree will decompose more quickly than those in the open, encouraged by the heat produced by the tree. In the absence of trees, deposit feces near a boulder. Thoughtful winter campers ski-pack a trail to a satisfactory spot (or more than one spot, to prevent an accumulation of feces) before they need the spot. Whenever possible, choose a spot where sunlight will hasten decomposition. Don't bury feces deeply in snow; a shallow hole, covered when you've finished, allows for a faster decomposition rate while still hiding the waste from sight. Although the melting snow in spring will soften and disperse the nasty mass, sunlight does most of the work of decomposition. Winter also offers the possibility of letting feces freeze, packing the piles in garbage bags, and sledding them out with you.

The use of toilet paper is acceptable, as long as you pack the soiled paper out. Snow makes a very nice natural wipe, if its consistency allows you to mold it into a usable shape.

Urination causes little or no harm to the environment in winter, but designating an appropriate spot eliminates the unsightliness of yellow holes all over the place. Locating that spot near a tree minimizes the possibility of gathering "bad" snow to melt for water.

LEAVE WHAT YOU FIND

Archaeological and historical artifacts are reminders of our rich human history, and they belong to all people for all time. Structures, dwellings, and artifacts on public lands are protected by the Archaeological Resources Protection Act and the National Historic Preservation Act and should not be disturbed. Snow buries many natural things, but not all things, and natural objects should likewise be left behind. If you want a souvenir, take a photograph, or draw a picture, and cherish the memories.

MINIMIZE CAMPFIRE IMPACT

Fires are not a usual part of winter trips, as good, dry wood is not always available, and low-impact fires can be difficult to pull off in deep snow. If they are practical and acceptable, however, build a minimum-impact fire. Use only dead and downed wood no thicker than your wrist. Keep the fire small. Burn all the wood down to ash, and then saturate the ash with water and scatter it broadly. When possible, use a gravel bar in the bed of an intermittent stream as the site for a fire—the spring runoff will remove small debris left over from the site (small amounts of charcoal are generally considered safe, even beneficial, to the environment). An uprooted tree may also provide exposed mineral soil, which is acceptable for a Leave No Trace fire. Get rid of all evidence of the fire before heading out.

RESPECT WILDLIFE

Wild animals are weaker and less well-fed in the winter than in warmer months, and thus are more likely to be harmed by contact with humans. Animals depend on the low-calorie food available in winter for all their warmth, and they cannot afford the energy lost if they are frightened and forced to flee. Observe wildlife quietly from a distance. Avoid quick movements and direct eye contact, actions that may be interpreted as aggression. Do not, intentionally or unintentionally (by leaving trash or storing food inappropriately), feed wildlife. If animals are changing their behavior because of you, change your behavior so they don't have to. Be especially considerate during those times that are toughest for animals: when the snow is deep; when the snow is covered with an icy crust that breaks under their weight, draining their energy and sometimes cutting their legs; and in spring, when their fat reserves are depleted.

BE CONSIDERATE OF OTHER VISITORS

You "own" the wilderness, along with millions of others, and they, too, deserve respect. The little things are often the most important. Simple courtesies—offering a friendly greeting on the trail, stepping aside to let stronger skiers pass, avoiding the destruction of a well-laid ski track, preserving the quiet—all make a difference. Practice trail etiquette. Lend a hand, if appropriate, to help those ahead. If possible, camp away from trails and other visitors.

Resources

AVALANCHE SAFETY

Daffern, Tony. *Avalanche Safety for Skiers & Climbers*. Calgary, Alberta, Canada: Rocky Mountain Books, 1983.

Fredston, Jill A., and Doug Fesler. *Snow Sense: A Guide to Evaluating Snow Avalanche Hazard*. Anchorage, AK: Arctic Environmental Information and Data Center, 1985.

CLOTHING

Giesbrecht, Gordon G. *Cold Weather Clothing*. A presentation at the Winter Wilderness Medicine Conference, Jackson, WY, February 2003. Available at www.umanitoba.ca/faculties/physed/research/people/giesbrecht/

FOOD AND NUTRITION

Howley, Mary. *NOLS Nutrition Field Guide*. Lander, WY: National Outdoor Leadership School, 2002.

Pearson, Claudia, ed. *NOLS Cookery*, 5th ed. Mechanicsburg, PA: Stackpole Books, 2004.

LEAVE NO TRACE

Hampton, Bruce, and David Cole. *NOLS Soft Paths: How to Enjoy the Wilderness without Harming It*, 3d ed. Mechanicsburg, PA: Stackpole Books, 1995.

Leave No Trace Center for Outdoor Ethics. 800-332-4100. www.LNT.org.

MOUNTAINEERING
Powers, Phil. *NOLS Wilderness Mountaineering.* Mechanicsburg, PA: Stackpole Books, 1993.

SKIING THE BACKCOUNTRY
O'Bannon, Allen, and Mike Clelland. *Allen & Mike's Really Cool Backcountry Ski Book: Traveling and Camping Skills for a Winter Environment.* Helena, MT: Falcon Publishing, 1996.

O'Bannon, Allen, and Mike Clelland. *Allen & Mike's Really Cool Telemark Tips: 109 Amazing Tips to Improve Your Tele-skiing.* Helena, MT: Falcon Publishing, 1998.

Parker, Paul. *Free-Heel Skiing.* Chelsea, VT: Chelsea Green Publishing, 1988.

WEATHER
National Oceanographic and Atmospheric Administration (NOAA). www.noaa.gov.

Williams, Jack. *The Weather Book: An Easy to-Understand Guide to the USA's Weather.* New York: Vintage Books, 1992.

WILDERNESS MEDICINE
Schimelpfenig, Tod, and Linda Lindsey. *NOLS Wilderness First Aid,* 3d ed. Mechanicsburg, PA: Stackpole Books, 2000.

Tilton, Buck. *Wilderness First Responder.* Guilford, CT: Globe Pequot Press, 2004.

Tilton, Buck, and Rick Bennett. *Don't Get Sick: The Hidden Dangers of Camping and Hiking.* Guilford, CT: Globe Pequot Press, 2002.

Wilderness Medicine Institute of NOLS, 284 Lincoln Street, Lander, WY 82520. 307-332-7800; 866-831-9001. http://wmi.nols.edu.

Glossary

blizzard: a storm with winds of at least thirty-five miles per hour and considerable falling or blowing snow, reducing visibility to less than one-quarter mile, lasting at least three hours; extremely cold temperatures are often associated with blizzard conditions but are not a formal part of the definition

boot-pack: to pack down snow by walking around with boots on

carabiners: metal links with gates that snap closed

chink: to fill cracks, such as between snow blocks in an igloo

condensation: the process of water vapor becoming liquid

cornice: windblown deposition of snow on a ridgetop that overhangs leeward

couloir: a steep gully filled with snow

creep: the tendency of snow to flow downhill

deadman: anything used as a weight buried in the snow to provide extra stability to a tent

dendrite: a hexagonal ice crystal with complex and often fern-like branches

depth hoar: snow buried in the snowpack that has metamorphosed into a weakly bonded layer

dew point: the air temperature at which vapor becomes liquid

evaporation: the process of liquid changing into vapor

facet: a new crystal formed in an existing snowpack

fall line: the route a falling object takes down a slope

glide: the tendency of snow to slide down a slope

hail: precipitation in the form of balls of solid ice

leeward: the side away from the prevailing wind; opposite of windward

metamorphosis: change in the structure and texture of snow crystals that results from variations in temperature, the migration of liquid water and water vapor, and pressure within the snow cover

penitente: old snow sun-sculpted into high, sharp points or edges

postholing: sinking up to the knees or higher in soft snow

rime: ice that forms from the freezing of a supercooled liquid when it makes contact with a subfreezing surface; forms on the windward side of objects

run-out: area at the bottom of a slope; area into which skiers or climbers will slide if they lose control during the ascent or descent of a slope

sastrugi: old, hard snow that is wind-sculpted into sometimes fantastic shapes

sintering: a process in which snow crystals are frozen together, "hardening" that snow

ski-pack: to pack down snow by walking around with skis on (ski-packed snow is not as dense as boot-packed snow)

sleet: precipitation in the form of balls of ice crystals with a hard shell and a soggy center

snow density: the mass of snow per unit volume

snow depth: the combined total depth of old and new snow on the ground

snowfall: the depth of new snow that has accumulated since the previous day or since the previous observation

snow flurries: snow that falls for short durations and often changes in intensity, usually producing little accumulation

snow load: downward force on an object or structure caused by the weight of accumulated snow

snowpack: the total snow and ice on the ground, including new snow, old snow, and ice that has not melted

sublimation: the process of ice changing directly to water vapor without melting, or vice versa

supercooled: the condition of a liquid when it remains in the liquid state even though its temperature is below its freezing point

surface hoar: loosely bonded ice crystals deposited on a surface

windslab: a slab of firm snow deposited from windblown particles

windward: side from which the wind is blowing; opposite of leeward

work-harden: to churn snow, breaking up the particles and then crunching them together, after which sintering causes the snow to get firmer

Index

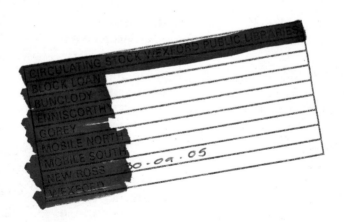